Easy Walks
in the
Cape Peninsula

CW00531677

Lawrence
Friarfield
London Road, Stamford
Lincs PE9 3JS
Tel. 01780-480255
Fax 01780-755289

MIKE LUNDY

Easy Walks
in the
Cape Peninsula

HUMAN & ROUSSEAU
Cape Town   Pretoria   Johannesburg

Dedicated to
The kindest and most considerate person I have met.
Somehow she manages to combine these gentle qualities
with a strong presence and compelling personality, which
draws people to her. Barbara, my friend, my lover and
my wife.

"Age is between the left ear and the right ear."
Hawk McGinnis
(70-year-old round-the-world walker)

"Idle people have the least leisure."
English Proverb

Visit Mike Lundy's website on
www.hikecapetown.co.za

First edition 1997
Second edition 1998
Third edition 2000
Fourth edition 2002
Fifth edition 2003
Fifth edition, second impression 2004

Copyright © 1997 by Mike Lundy
First published by Human & Rousseau
40 Heerengracht, Cape Town
Front cover: Returning from the Noon Gun, Signal Hill.
Cover design by Chérie Collins
Typeset in 11 on 13 pt New Baskerville by ALINEA STUDIO
Printed and bound by Paarl Print,
Oosterland Street, Paarl, South Africa

ISBN 0 7981 4363 0

ACKNOWLEDGEMENTS

I have ruthlessly picked the brains of many knowledgeable people to write this book. I am also deeply indebted to a number of others who willingly gave their help and advice. My very sincere thanks to:

Rijer van der Vlugt and Greg Forsythe of the Mountain Club of South Africa for their advice in the planning stages.
David McKelly, Lynn Carelse and Reney Robyntjies of the CSIR who updated, refurbished and printed the maps for me.
Jim Hallinan from the Cape of Good Hope Nature Reserve.
Tom Keane of the Fish Hoek Alien Vegetation Control Group.
Peter Salter of the Simon's Town Flora Conservation Group.
Dr Gerard Malan of the Agricultural Research Council at Elsenburg.
Cape Union Mart for their promotion of my books and hiking gear.
My wife, Barbara, and secretary, Sue Lucas, for mountains of typing.
Wally Petersen of the Kommetjie Environmental Action Group.
Professor William Bond and Dr Dave Richardson of the Botany Department at UCT.
Professor John Hoffmann of the Zoology Department at UCT.
The Lighthouse Services Division of Portnet.
Dr Phil Hockey of the Ornithology Department at UCT.
Dr Tony Williams of Cape Nature Conservation.
Cmdr. Gerry de Vries and Lieut. Braam Krause of the SA Navy.
Dr Mike Morris of the Plant Protection Research Institute.
Margaret Cartwright of the Simon's Town Museum.
Liz Wheeler of the Friends of the Liesbeek.
Howard Langley of the National Parks Board.
Mark Hawthorne of the Parks and Forests Branch for taking me to Hell's Gates and back.
My editor Linette Viljoen.
. . . and anyone else I might have unintentionally left out.

Maps funded by courtesy of Cape Union Mart and based on the digital footpath database, belonging to the Mountain Club of South Africa. My sincere thanks to both.

CONTENTS

FOREWORD

Through his earlier writings Mike Lundy has provided an invaluable service to Capetonians and to visitors.

Easy Walks in the Cape Peninsula is yet another major contribution towards introducing all the wonderful opportunities for full enjoyment of our city.

Table Mountain is a "must" for every visitor to Cape Town. The Cape Peninsula and its famous mountain chain already feature among South Africa's top tourist attractions. Capetonians have every reason to be proud of this world-renowned natural asset. It is sad, though, that it is too often taken for granted. Sadly, too, there are many people living in view of the mountain chain who, for a variety of reasons, have never been able to ascend its heights or just simply to enjoy the many walks on its slopes. Mike Lundy's latest book serves to bring the mountain and the Peninsula's walks to all who live and visit here.

For those who have not yet enjoyed our natural heritage, this book will be an incentive to step out of the great bustling city of Cape Town into the natural wilderness, right here on our doorstep. For those already familiar with the many trails on offer to the public, this book will provide an even greater choice of routes to follow. It will also widen and expand their knowledge of the history and points of interest relevant to each trail and walk.

May this publication serve to encourage Capetonians and visitors to enrich their daily lives with the spiritual, emotional and physical refreshment to be experienced on these routes.

We can only express our gratitude to the author for producing this proud publication which should be a prized possession of residents and visitors alike.

GORDON OLIVER
Chief Executive, CAPTOUR, 1997

INTRODUCTION

The responses to my weekly radio talks and newspaper columns were very clear. There are a huge number of people out there who are armchair hikers. They would dearly love to get out and do it, but for one reason or another cannot face the dreadful prospect of actually having to spend some energy in the process! The top of a mountain is simply not negotiable in their minds, let alone their legs. But who says you have to go to the *top*? The Cape Peninsula is blessed with some of the most beautiful walks in the world. And many of them are on the level. Magnificent scenery and unspoilt nature are at our very doorstep, and all it needs is for someone to show you where, with a promise of minimum effort for maximum return. This book, I hope, is just such a promise.

I have a mission. A mission to lead people to beautiful places. But more importantly, to teach them to appreciate those beautiful places and come away from them all the richer for the experience. To say to themselves, "I learnt something interesting I didn't know before, and I would like to protect this place for my children's children to appreciate."

With more and more people filling less and less space on earth, we need to preserve our recreational areas now more than ever. To save our mountains, we need to educate and educate and educate.

Even one toffee paper or cigarette end is a blight on the face of our beautiful mountain. The words of Chief Seatlh (Seattle) to the early North American settlers are worth thinking about:

"All things are connected
Whatever befalls the earth
befalls the sons of the earth.
This we know.

The earth does not belong to man.
Man belongs to the earth.
This we know.

Man does not weave the web of life.
He is merely a strand in it.
Whatever he does to the web
he does to himself."

I sincerely hope you are tempted to arise from your metaphorical armchair, stroll through nature and history on a voyage of discovery, and be amazed at the beauty which has always surrounded you. Tighten your muscles and relax your soul.

MIKE LUNDY
September 1997

STARTING OUT

Although the terms are often used to mean the same thing, there is more than a subtle difference between hiking, backpacking and mountaineering. Loosely speaking, a hiker carries a daypack and comes home at night. A backpacker carries his bed and a mountaineer is attached to his fellow climbers by rope – and preferably to the cliff face as well. It's all a matter of to what degree you wish to expose yourself.

Clearly you wish to come home at night, otherwise you wouldn't have bought this book. Rule Number One if you don't wish to expose yourself, but come home at night, is to carry extra clothing and rain gear. This should be *regardless* of how favourable the weather might be when you start. The Cape Peninsula is infamous for sudden, dramatic changes in the weather. I *always* carry rain gear and a jersey, even in midsummer.

To carry these things, along with your water bottle, you will need a daypack. If you are a beginner, a basic 20-25-litre daypack will suffice. You can graduate to a 75-litre backpack when you are ready, if ever, to sleep under a rock overhang or in a bats' cave.

Next on your shopping list should be a pair of lightweight fabric boots. Only think about the more expensive heavy-duty leather boots if you decide to take your hiking more seriously.

Either way, ankle support is important, not only to prevent twisted ankles, but also to hold the foot back in the boot and avoid toe blisters on the downhills. When buying boots, try them on with a pair of thick socks (preferably 100% wool). You should be able to fit two fingers between your heel and the unlaced boot. Toe space is all-important if you want to avoid blisters. Be sure to insist on non-slip soles, of which two excellent makes are REP and VIBRAM.

Never wear nylon socks. Nylon does not absorb sweat and will probably lead to blisters or chafing. If you need to wear two pairs of socks, wear pure cotton underneath pure wool: stick to natural fibres and they won't stick to you.

Lastly – if you think you are hooked – join a club. At the last count there were a couple of dozen to choose from in the greater Cape Town area (see pages 184-5.).

THE TEN COMMANDMENTS OF MOUNTAIN SAFETY

(Modified and condensed from guidelines by the Mountain Club of South Africa)

1. **Never climb alone**. Four is the ideal party.
2. **Choose your route** according to the **ability, fitness** and **experience** of the group.
3. **Use a guidebook,** or go with somebody who **genuinely** knows the way.
4. Ensure that at least one member of the group has a **fully charged cellphone**.
5. **Always** go prepared for **bad weather**.
6. Tell someone **exactly** where you are going and **stick to this plan**.
7. **Travel at the pace of the slowest** member of the party.
8. **Never split up** and go in different directions.
9. **Do not push on into the unknown**. If you get lost, retrace your steps.
10. If you are unsure of what to do, **find shelter**, especially from the wind, and **stay put**.

A FLORAL PARADISE UNDER THREAT

If you are to walk the mountains and footpaths of the Cape Peninsula, then you need to know that you are in the botanical treasure house of the world. And very few Capetonians are even aware of it. The globe is divided into six botanical regions – each one called a Floral Kingdom. The Cape Floral Kingdom is one of those six, and is far and away the smallest in area (only 0,04% of the total). It is also far and away the richest in plant life. In the Cape Peninsula alone there are more species of flowering plants than in the whole of Great Britain. Europe boasts of having 21 species of *Erica* heath. Their heather is well known, especially in Scotland, splashing the countryside with colour. But in the Western Cape, we have no fewer than 657 species of *Erica*; a concentration unequalled by any other plant group in the world.

And ericas are just one of the three main components of fynbos, the other two being the protea family and the restios (reeds).

That's the good news.

The Bad News

Our treasure trove is under serious threat from alien plant invaders. Only 40% of the fynbos flora found here in Van Riebeeck's time has survived, and still we are the richest botanical region on earth. But not for long, unless the alien vegetation is brought under control and prevented from smothering the indigenous plants.

The Economic Effect

Why worry? you might ask. Green is green. Who cares what form it takes?

The economic effect of a takeover by alien plants is devastating. They choke dams and rivers, destabilize river banks and cause soil erosion and silting up of estuaries. Perhaps the most costly effect of alien vegetation is that these plants and trees rob us of our much-needed water before it even reaches the dams – requiring even more dams to be built. Alien trees can drink many times more water than indigenous fynbos. And where there might have been five hundred species of indigenous flowering plants, now there is just one – an alien. Witness for example the floor of a pine forest, or a blue gum forest, a thicket of rooikrans, hakea or Port Jackson. They are totally selfish, to the exclusion of all else.

The Main Culprits

Public Enemy No. 1 is the black wattle (*Acacia mearnsii*). Unfortunately it's the highest-paying timber crop in the country, so commercial interests are powerful. It produces a high yield of tannin (used in the tanning industry) and rayon is produced from the wood chips. On the other side of the coin, due to its shallow roots, it causes river banks to wash away, with resultant flooding and devastation downstream.

Other botanical pirates and plunderers which pose a serious threat, are pines and hakea in the mountains and rooikrans (*Acacia cyclops*) in the lowlands. Two that were a serious problem, Port Jackson (*Acacia saligna*) and the long-leaved wattle (*Acacia longifolia*), are on their way out, thanks to a highly effective biological control programme (see below).

Biological Governors

These alien plants were introduced in the first place for a variety of reasons, including fuel, forestry, sand stabilization, shade, etc. Unfortunately their biological governors were left behind in their countries of origin (mainly Australia). The reason they became problems was that they came from areas with a similar climate, but here found no natural enemies. As a result, seed production was far greater and they spread remorselessly across the country, wiping out everything in their path.

The Solution

Enthusiastic hack groups serve a valuable educational purpose. But in my opinion they hardly scratch the surface of the problem when it comes to removing it for good. The only long-term answer is biological control.

Recently there have been a couple of spectacular successes which, if you walk the mountain, you cannot avoid noticing.

The Port Jackson willow (*Acacia saligna*) is being systematically wiped out by a rust fungus (*Uromycladium tepperianum*) imported from Australia. Notice what a friend of mine rather coarsely refers to as "flying elephant turds", hanging from the branches of the Port Jackson. The fungus causes the cells of the host tree to multiply and enlarge in a "cancerous" type of growth, and also taps into the vascular system. Rather like an arboreal vampire, it sucks the tree to death.

Another success story belongs to the gall wasp, also imported from Down Under, to control the long-leaved wattle (*Acacia longifolia*).

This amazing little insect only lives for three or four days, during which time it must find a very specific host – the long-leaved wattle. It lays its 15 to 20 eggs in the flower bud in January, where they remain dormant until September; a time when the bud would normally become a flower. Then the eggs hatch and the larvae secrete a chemical which mimics one of the plant's hormones, causing it to produce callused tissue around the larvae. This aborts the flower and gives the larvae a wonderful home in the form of a tough green berry-like gall. The larvae pupate and by January turn into adult wasps, which chew their way out of the gall. *The tree has effectively been persuaded to produce wasps instead of seeds!* Each wasp then has just three or four days to go in search of a suitable flower in which to lay its eggs and repeat the cycle.

The adults are mostly females (90%) and can produce progeny without mating. This is a somewhat distressing concept for us mere males.

The Moral of the Story

Be proud of what we have in the Western Cape and be aware of the threat. Education will eventually eradicate it, with the help of the gall wasp, the rust fungus and other friends.

TABLE MOUNTAIN NATIONAL PARK

Proclaimed in 1998, they are the custodians of the Cape Peninsula mountain chain. Their stated vision is "**A park for all, forever**". They work in close partnership with the City of Cape Town and are generously funded by the Mother City. Because of the enormous threat to the biodiversity of the region, much emphasis and funds were dedicated to the clearing of alien vegetation. Now that this battle is nearly won, more energy will be spent on footpaths and upgrades.

DOGS

The TMNP requires that all hikers wishing to walk their dogs in permitted areas under their control, need to be in possession of a Wild Card. Further details from (021) 701-8692.

THE CAPE PENINSULA

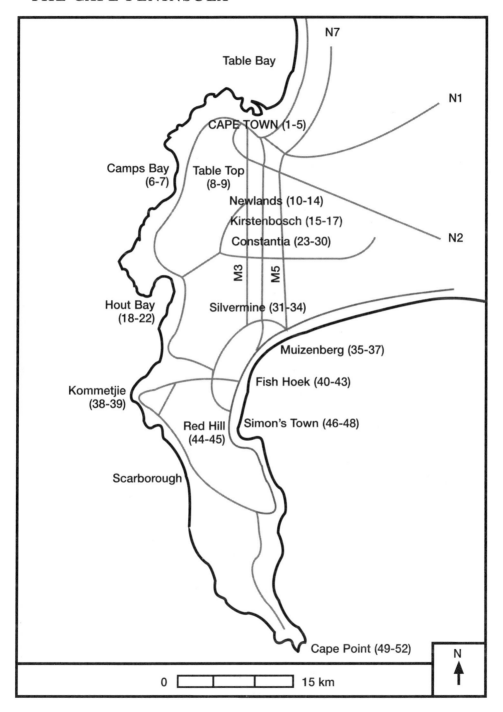

Table Bay

N7

N1

CAPE TOWN (1-5)

Camps Bay (6-7)

Table Top (8-9)

Newlands (10-14)

Kirstenbosch (15-17)

Constantia (23-30)

N2

M3

M5

Hout Bay (18-22)

Silvermine (31-34)

Muizenberg (35-37)

Fish Hoek (40-43)

Kommetjie (38-39)

Red Hill (44-45)

Simon's Town (46-48)

Scarborough

Cape Point (49-52)

N

0   15 km

1. THE LION'S RUMP

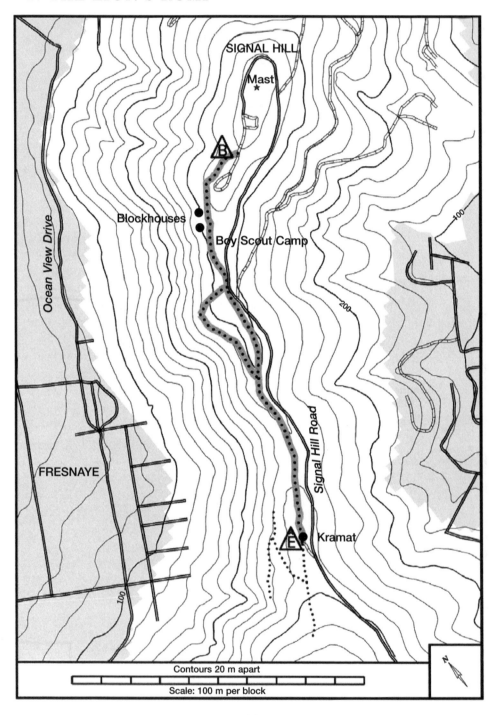

SIGNAL HILL

Mast

B

Blockhouses

Boy Scout Camp

Ocean View Drive

FRESNAYE

Signal Hill Road

100

200

100

E

Kramat

100

N

Contours 20 m apart

Scale: 100 m per block

THE LION'S RUMP

1

Time: 25 minutes

Distance: 2,2 km

Route: One-way

Dogs allowed

Brief Description

A level walk along the lion's back, from the main parking area on Signal Hill to the Muslim tomb, with wonderful views over Sea Point on one side and the City Bowl on the other. If you do not wish to walk back, arrange to be picked up at the Kramat. No shade or water.

Start

Park your car at the main parking area and viewpoint at the very end of Signal Hill Road, leading from Kloof Nek. Begin your walk from the far right-hand corner of the parking area (Lion's Head/Sea Point corner).

Directions

The concrete path crosses a neat lawn and picnic area before dipping down onto a rough gravel path. Ahead of you, directly in line with Lion's Head, you will see the bright green roof of the Kramat – your destination.

One hundred metres beyond the lawns, the path takes you just to the left of another picnic area with concrete tables and stools. This one is perhaps more pleasant than its lawned counterpart at the start, due to the shade provided by some rather unexpected trees. Clearly they have been planted there by the authorities, for who would expect to find Outeniqua yellow-woods (*Podocarpus falcatus*), sweet thorn (*Acacia karroo*), wild peach (*Kiggelaria africana*) and wild olive (*Olea africana*) on Signal Hill? And fine specimens they are too, even if they might be somewhat confused about their surroundings.

Continue past the left-hand side of this little indigenous grove and suddenly you will be presented with a breathtaking view as Fresnaye and Sea Point open up before you. Five or six minutes after starting you will come to the corner of a fenced property belonging to the

Boy Scouts and used as a camp. The path follows the fence down its length before spilling onto a parking area. Note the old Defence Force blockhouses below the path to the right (see Points of Interest).

The path continues from the far end of the parking place which serves the Scout Camp. Note there are two paths; one leading off each corner. Take the right-hand one as it gives a spectacular view of the Sea Point coastline. You could be forgiven for imagining Argentina is just below the western horizon! If you choose to walk back, return via the left-hand path, which gives a view over the City Bowl.

Five minutes along either path will meet up again with the other and then continue as a single path for another 10 minutes, before reaching the Kramat. If you enter the Dargan, treat it as a holy place and respect the Muslim custom of removing your shoes.

Points of Interest

❀ The abandoned and derelict Defence Force blockhouses just below the Scout Camp were part of a series of outposts making up the coastal defences of the Cape Peninsula during the Second World War. The larger one was probably the Operations Room from where they could direct the fire of the guns from the Lion Battery above the Harbour, Fort Wynyard next to the V&A Waterfront and the Apostle Battery at Llandudno.

❀ The Kramat or Muslim tomb is one of many dotted around the Peninsula. This one is the final resting place of Hassan Gaibe Sha Al Quadri.

THE NOON GUN

2

Time: 20 minutes down/30 minutes up

Distance: 1,1 km or 2,2 km

Route: One-way or return

Dogs allowed

Brief Description

A moderately steep gravel road which leads through uninteresting vegetation but provides wonderful views along its route. You will be treated to aerial views of Green Point Common followed by the V&A Waterfront, the Foreshore and Harbour and finally Schotsekloof. The walk ends at the fascinating Lion Battery, from which Cape Town's world-famous noon gun is fired.

Should you not wish to climb back uphill to your car, arrange for someone to pick you up. However, to get to Lion Battery by car is considerably further than walking it. (Proceed back to Kloof Nek, and down into town to Buitengracht Street. Get onto the elevated road above Buitengracht Street. Off this elevated Buitengracht Street leads Whitford Street. Follow that to the very top where it becomes Military Road, going off to the right. Then follow Military Road for 1,2 km to the Lion Battery.)

Start

From the main parking area at the very end of Signal Hill Road, leading off from Kloof Nek. Begin your walk from just to the right of the public toilets, situated off the near left-hand corner of the parking area.

Directions

The path down from the parking area leads you back to the road you have just driven up. Cross over it and directly opposite is a boom blocking the entrance to a jeep track. Follow this jeep track down the slope for about 10 minutes, after which you will come to a side road going sharply back to your left. Take this and follow it down to the perimeter fence of the Lion Battery, then follow this fence down to the gate below.

19

2. THE NOON GUN

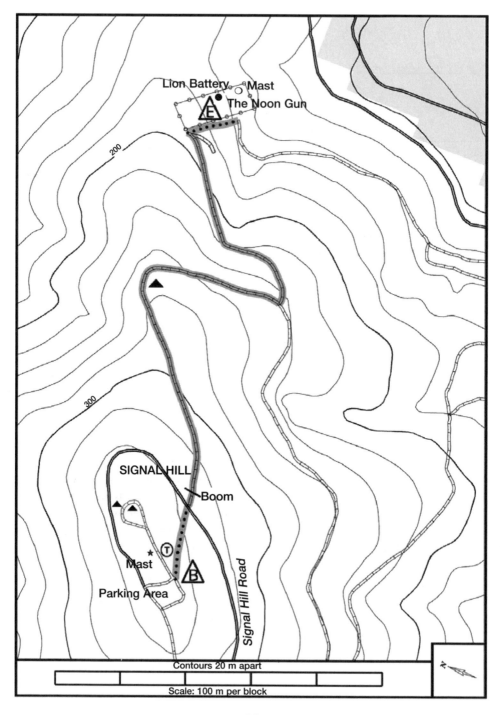

Lion Battery   Mast
The Noon Gun

SIGNAL HILL
Boom

Mast
Parking Area

Signal Hill Road

Contours 20 m apart

Scale: 100 m per block

N

Points of Interest

❁ The noon gun is fired every day except Sundays and Public Holidays and the battery is open to the public between 11h00 and 13h00 Monday to Saturday.

❁ Although the Lion Battery was only completed in 1890, the tradition of firing a noon gun in Cape Town has been around since 1806, when it was fired from the Imhoff Battery at the Castle. When the city began to expand, it was moved to its present site on 4 August 1902.

❁ The gun is fired electronically from The Observatory in Observatory at precisely 12 noon. It has an atomic clock with an accuracy close to one millionth of a second. Such incredible accuracy, however, is no longer needed. In the not so far off days when ships depended heavily on the accuracy of their chronometers for navigation, Cape Town's noon gun had the very practical purpose of allowing ships in the bay to reset their timepieces accurately. However, as the sound would take six or seven seconds to reach them in the bay (representing a huge error in navigational terms) the gunpowder is formulated to give off a large puff of smoke, so that noon is when you see it, not when you hear it. One indignant old gentleman living in Milnerton phoned the Lion Battery to tell them that they are consistently 11 seconds late in firing the noon gun. He cited the BBC pips as his evidence. It must have been somewhat deflating to be told that the sound takes consistently 11 seconds to reach Milnerton!

❁ The only other cities in the world that fire a daily noon gun are Hong Kong, Nice and Rome, but all these are fairly recent innovations.

❁ Two guns are loaded daily with a 1,36-kg charge of gunpowder in a cotton bag, which fits comfortably into the hand. It was surprising to me that such a small bag could make such a deafening bang! The second gun is a stand-by in case the first one misfires.

❁ The four guns in a row at the perimeter of the battery are used for 21 gun salutes. Again, one is on stand-by while the other three fire seven rounds each alternately, at five-second intervals.

❁ In 1997 a 27-metre naval mast was erected to commemorate the 75th anniversary of the founding of the South African Navy.

3. FRONTAL CONTOUR PATH

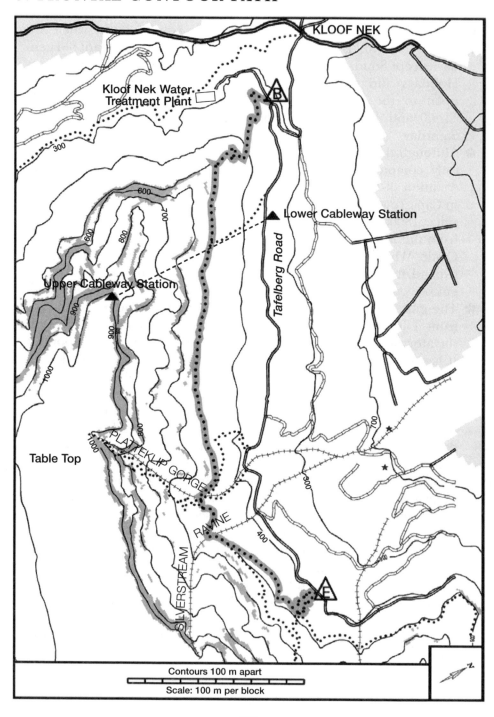

KLOOF NEK

Kloof Nek Water Treatment Plant

B

300

600

700

600

800

900

900

Upper Cableway Station

Lower Cableway Station

Tafelberg Road

1000

800

PLATTEKLIP GORGE

Table Top

1000

RAVINE

SILVERSTREAM

300

400

700

E

Contours 100 m apart

Scale: 100 m per block

N

FRONTAL CONTOUR PATH

3

CITY BOWL

Time: 2 hours 15 minutes

Distance: 4,3 km

Route: One-way

Dogs allowed

Brief Description

The first half-hour of this walk requires a bit of effort to get up to the level of the Contour Path running along the base of Table Mountain, overlooking the City Bowl. Once on the level path it is an easy stroll, with panoramic views of the city. The route takes you under the cableway and later into the pleasant and shady Silverstream Ravine, worthy of a tea break, just before your zigzag descent back down to Tafelberg Road. If you were to follow the Contour Path to its natural conclusion, it would lead you all the way to Constantia Nek. But don't try that unless you're prepared to walk for seven hours!

Start

0,8 km from Kloof Nek on the way to the lower cable station. Find parking near the second hairpin bend in the road. The path starts just to the left of the entrance gates to the Kloof Nek Water Treatment Plant. Your second car should be waiting at the end of the hike (unless you want to walk back). This is a further 3,2 km along Tafelberg Road from the start, past the lower cable station and at a point where there are blue gums on both sides of the road, with a parking area on the left, opposite a Table Mountain sign and the zigzag path down from the Saddle. If you have too many people to travel in one car, leave some at the start.

Directions

Take the path just to the left and outside of the gates to the Kloof Nek Water Treatment Plant. The path rises gently at first, becoming steeper as you get closer to your first goal – the beginning of the Contour Path, marked by the trig beacon on the corner, at the base of the cliff face above you.

It is most encouraging to see

the steps are made from recycled plastic – certainly the only plastic welcome on the mountain. Remember to take your plastic bags back home with you. They might eventually become steps on the mountain instead of an unsightly mess.

On reaching the Contour Path, walk just a few metres to the right to the trig beacon for your well-earned rest. From this point you will look down onto Camps Bay, Balie Bay and Bakoven. The large red-roofed building directly below is the water treatment plant.

After getting back your breath, set out in the direction of Devil's Peak along the Contour Path. After about 10 minutes you will meet the steep rocky steps coming up from the lower cable station and a few minutes later pass under the cableway.

The clearly defined layers to the sandstone all around you, and on which you are walking, are testimony to the sedimentary origins of this rock (see Points of Interest).

After about 45 minutes of walking along the level Contour Path, it will bend sharply around to the right and into Platteklip Gorge (at its top end it forms the "nick" in the Table Top). On a busy weekend, the number of people going up Platteklip Gorge might remind one of St George's Mall at lunch time. Despite being a most unpleasant way up or down (steep with no water or shade) it remains the most popular and most accessible climb to the Table Top. Due to the high traffic up and down, you could almost get run over here if you sit down for tea. So rather carry on to the next ravine, a few short minutes further on. This is done by crossing over the stream of Platteklip Gorge and continuing for about 100 m before coming to a sign pointing the way up Platteklip Gorge. Don't be tempted to follow the masses. Rather continue along this Contour Path and follow the signpost to Devil's Peak. Silverstream Ravine is just around the corner and provides both shelter and shade underneath a rock overhang, as well as shelter from the wind. It also has water all year round.

After suitable refreshment, continue along your way. Just two minutes past Silverstream Ravine, you will come to a fork in the path. Keep left and start your descent to your car which you will soon see below. At a meeting of four ways, take the only unlabelled route down the zigzag path to the road below.

Points of Interest
❀ Balie Bay between Camps Bay and Bakoven, as seen from the

trig beacon, has an unusual origin to its name. I had always thought it was Barley Bay until I saw it spelt. Then I was determined to find its origin, which rather ignominiously lies in a sewage pipe. The old Camps Bay sewage outfall entered the sea here and one Afrikaans word for a night soil bucket is a less euphemistic and more direct *kakbalie*. Hence Balie Bay.

✿ The sedimentary rock which forms the bulk of Table Mountain was deposited in layers from above in ancient seas. As a raised geological feature Table Mountain is relatively young at 60 million years old. The precursor of Table Mountain was at least six times its present height.

✿ The cableway passes up India Ravine, so named because it forms the outline of a map of India when seen from the city.

✿ Africa Ravine, to the left of it, is similarly named, as it resembles – perhaps not quite as accurately – the map of Africa.

4. WOODSTOCK CAVE

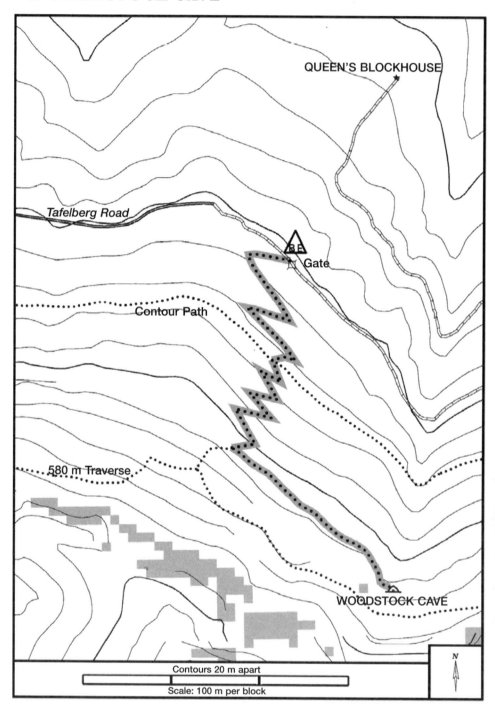

QUEEN'S BLOCKHOUSE

Tafelberg Road

B.B.

Gate

Contour Path

580 m Traverse

WOODSTOCK CAVE

N

Contours 20 m apart

Scale: 100 m per block

WOODSTOCK CAVE 4

Time: 30 minutes up/20 minutes down

Distance: 1,6 km

Route: Return

Dogs allowed

Brief Description

Once you know the position of Woodstock Cave on Devil's Peak, you will forever find yourself looking for the dark slit in the face of Devil's Peak. It is clearly visible from the Foreshore, Paarden Eiland and surrounding areas. The climb is a short series of zigzags along a path which is rough underfoot, so be sure to wear appropriate boots. The cave is a substantial rock overhang 50 m wide by 15 m deep and three or four metres high at the mouth. In winter a waterfall flows over the centre section of the opening. The panoramic view of Table Bay and the city from inside the cave is well worth a picture.

Start

Drive exactly 5 km beyond the lower cable station along Tafelberg Road to the end of the tarred section. Then a further 100 m on dirt road will get you to a metal gate with stone pillars. The start of the climb is well hidden just 10 paces before the gate. The yellow-brown rocky face hides the beginning of the path.

Directions

The path zigzags its way slowly up the slope. After four zigzags, the path eventually reaches a contour path which encircles the mountain all the way from Constantia Nek to Kloof Nek.

Cross over this important thoroughfare and start counting the zigzags again. Do not add to the already serious erosion problem by taking short cuts. After the seventh zigzag from the Contour Path you will be confronted with a steep log step and rock scramble. About 10 m before reaching this steep section, take a side path cutting back in the direction from which you have just come. You should now be more or less level with the cave. A few short minutes

27

will bring you to its mouth. Retrace your steps to return.

Points of Interest

❀ Mindless fools have seen fit to carry pots of paint up here to leave their names without any apparent shame, for all to see and despise. What is it that inspires the sick graffiti brigade to deface our natural heritage in this manner? I would like to think they are low-class people without culture or pride, but alas I suspect this may not be so. Maybe they are just ordinary people who need help from a psychiatrist.

THE KING'S BLOCKHOUSE

5

Time: 1 hour 15 minutes

Distance: 3,1 km

Route: Circular

Dogs allowed

Brief Description

Apart from a ten-minute climb up a steep path, the rest is easy walking on the level. The outward route is along a gravel road, followed by the steep climb to reach the blockhouse, and the return route along the so-called Lower Traverse, an easy contour path with magnificent views of the city. The view from the King's Battery itself is all-commanding, as well it should be, considering its original purpose. There is no shade. Water is available from a concrete reservoir behind the blockhouse.

Start

On Tafelberg Road, exactly 5 km beyond the lower cable station. One hundred metres beyond where Tafelberg Road comes to an end, is a stone and iron gate across the gravel road.

Directions

Leave your car parked near the gate and walk through it. The gravel track will immediately take you into a grove of rather interesting trees. They are exotics and were obviously planted a long time ago. What makes them interesting is they have bark like a cork tree and acorns like an oak tree, but leaves unlike either. These apparent mongrels are called – not surprisingly – cork oaks.

Continue along the gravel road and notice, some way below, the ruins of the Queen's Blockhouse. On a weekend you might hear the sound of gunfire, which would be coming from the shooting range just above De Waal Drive to the right of the Queen's Blockhouse. The King's Blockhouse starts to peak out from the skyline ahead.

Some 20 minutes after starting, you will be joined by another gravel road from the left. Carry straight on for about 200 m past the fork to a point beyond some dead pine trees, where the road

29

5. THE KING'S BLOCKHOUSE

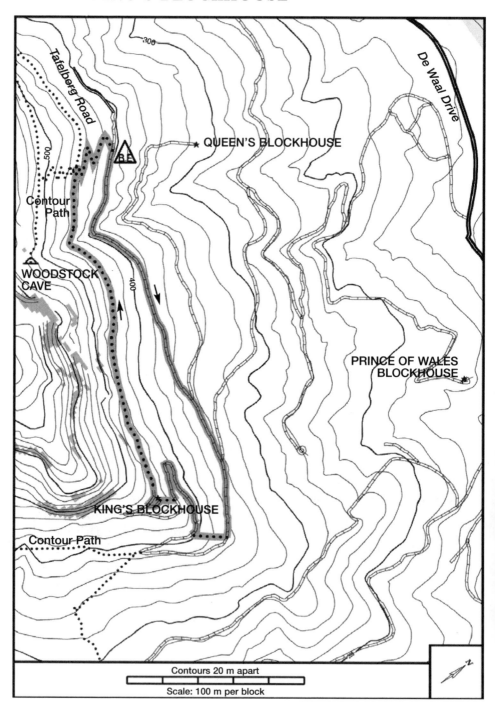

Tafelberg Road

300

QUEEN'S BLOCKHOUSE

500

B.E.

Contour
Path

WOODSTOCK
CAVE

400

PRINCE OF WALES
BLOCKHOUSE

KING'S BLOCKHOUSE

Contour Path

De Waal Drive

Contours 20 m apart

Scale: 100 m per block

N

begins to bend to the right. Look for a turnstile-type gate in the fence on the left. Directly opposite is a steep path going straight up the slope. Ten minutes of this upward slog will bring you back onto the gravel road. Turn right and follow the road for another seven or eight minutes where it brings you to a memorial to the forester who lived and worked here until 1895. His friends and colleagues praised him for covering these "barren slopes" with trees. They failed to mention they were invasive pine trees from Europe, which we are still trying to get rid of. However, one can't help envying him the superb view from his house over a hundred years ago. See how well you know Cape Town, and attempt to pick out landmarks such as the Liesbeek River, Rondebosch Common, Newlands rugby and cricket grounds, the airport, etc.

Pass the cannon a few metres further on and make your way up the slope to the blockhouse looming above. Pass to the right of it and on the slope just above is a small concrete circular reservoir, where you will always find water.

The steps going up past the reservoir lead to the top of Devil's Peak. Presumably you don't wish to be that energetic, so keep on the level to the right of and just a few metres below the reservoir.

This will be the beginning of your return route along the so-called Lower Traverse. After 10 minutes along this path enjoying the views of the City Bowl, you will be taken into a ravine. Look up and see Woodstock Cave directly above (see pages 26 to 28).

Once again the route bisects the line of cork oaks, this time at their top end. About 100 m beyond the cork oaks, a zigzag path comes up from the road below, on its way to Woodstock Cave. Take this path down and back to your car.

Points of Interest

❀ The King's Blockhouse is officially known on survey maps as the King's Battery and was built by the British during their first occupation of the Cape between 1795 and 1803. Its guns were never fired in anger, but at one time it was used to accommodate convict labour during afforestation of Devil's Peak.

❀ The Queen's, King's and Prince of Wales Blockhouses formed a trio of small forts built in 1797 to protect Cape Town against attack from the south – which is exactly the route the British themselves chose after the Battle of Muizenberg. They were not going to allow a repeat performance by an enemy.

6. CAMPS BAY – GREEN POINT CONTOUR

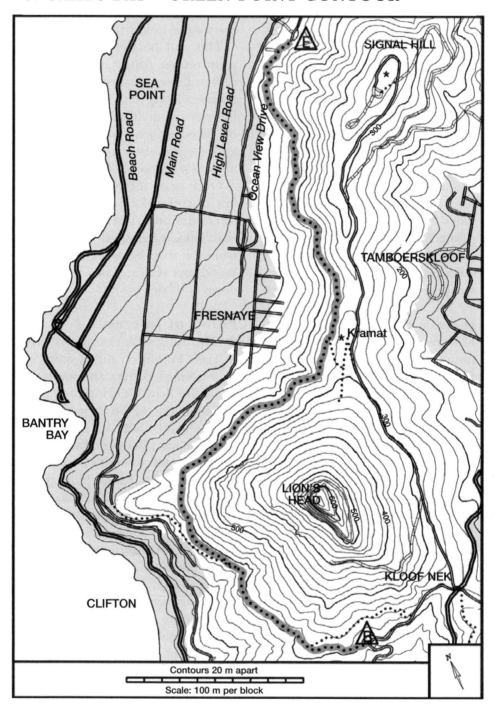

SIGNAL HILL

SEA
POINT

Beach Road

Main Road

High Level Road

Ocean View Drive

TAMBOERSKLOOF

FRESNAYE

Kramat

BANTRY
BAY

LION'S
HEAD

CLIFTON

KLOOF NEK

Contours 20 m apart

Scale: 100 m per block

N

CAMPS BAY – GREEN POINT CONTOUR

CAMPS BAY

Time: 1 hour 45 minutes

Distance: 4,9 km

Route: One-way

Dogs allowed

Brief Description

Only the first five minutes of this walk requires any effort. The rest is a delightfully scenic stroll, mostly on the level, overlooking our beautiful Sunset Coast. Lion's Head towers above you, with brooding grandeur.

I am reminded of Rio de Janeiro and the view of Copacobana from Corcovado. It might well be concrete, but it does have a certain magnetism.

Your first views on this walk, however, are not of concrete suburbia, but of the most amazing concentration of watsonias, which have sprung up with a vengeance after a devastating fire in 1995. In late spring and early summer they will be stunning. Then overlook the famous Clifton beaches, come uncomfortably close to the up-market mansions of upper Fresnaye, look down on the flatland of Sea Point and finally onto the green sportsfields of Green Point

Common. A rewarding walk without too much effort. You will need a car at each end, or someone to pick you up at a prearranged time. There is no water on the trail, so take sufficient with you.

Start

At the hairpin bend on the road from Kloof Nek to Clifton. End at the very top of Glengariff Road, Three Anchor Bay, where it joins the beginning of Springbok Road.

Directions

On the bend in the road, a steep path ascends the slope behind a Lion's Head signboard.

A rule of thumb for this walk is: when in doubt, keep right.

After ten to fifteen minutes look down on picturesque Clifton and wonder who had the total lack of imagination and sensitivity to name the beaches First, Second, Third and Fourth Beach. At least the two rocks a couple of kilometres out to sea from the blandly named beaches do have colourful names. They are South Paw on the left and North Paw on the right – for they are the paws of the lion on whose flank you are walking.

Fork to go above the blue gums ahead and not through them. Then a few minutes later, take the right-hand fork again through five vertical poles in the pathway. The path leads you close to the back of the top line of houses.

Thirty-five to forty minutes after starting you will come to a bench on a rock with a panoramic view over Sea Point. As this is not far off the halfway mark it would seem an appropriate place to rest and refresh.

Look up at the huge granite slab above and notice some alien palm trees growing rather unexpectedly out of some cracks in the rock.

Interestingly, above the slab is an entirely different rock type forming the main mass of Lion's Head. The granite base is igneous in origin, having been pushed up from below the earth's crust. The overlying sandstone which forms Lion's Head, however, is sedimentary in origin. That is to say it was formed from above, with layer upon layer of sediment dropping out onto the beds of ancient seas and rivers. You are looking at a history book of the earth.

Soon after starting on your way again you will bisect a line of blue gums, and fifteen minutes after your rest you will come to another bench, this time above the path. Immediately after that you will come to a T-junction. At this point turn left and stick to the clear path all the way back to your waiting second car, some 30-35 minutes away.

Points of Interest

❀ The Atlantic Suburbs took a long time to be developed. Van Riebeeck and his successors were far more drawn to the fertile ground surrounding the Liesbeek River. They were interested in vegetables, not vistas.

❀ The names of the places you will see on this walk have undergone an interesting metamorphosis over the years. Camps Bay was named after Frederich von Camptz, described by the Governor in the 1780s as "a troublesome and annoying person". He owned a farm in the area, and it became known as von Camptz Baai. Property developers around 1900 called it New Brighton and then finally anglicized the original name to Camps Bay.

❀ Look down on Clifton and try to imagine this delightful place with the name Schoenmakers-

34

gat. The person who lived there and after whom it was named, seems to have been as unpleasant as von Camptz. Adam Tas in his diary of 1697 relates the story of "Jacobus (the) Schoenmaker, scum of a cobbler and his cross-grained slut of a wife". Harsh words indeed. And such a nice place. Clifton almost certainly got its present name a century ago, from the owner of the original Clifton Hotel – Mrs Bess Clifton.

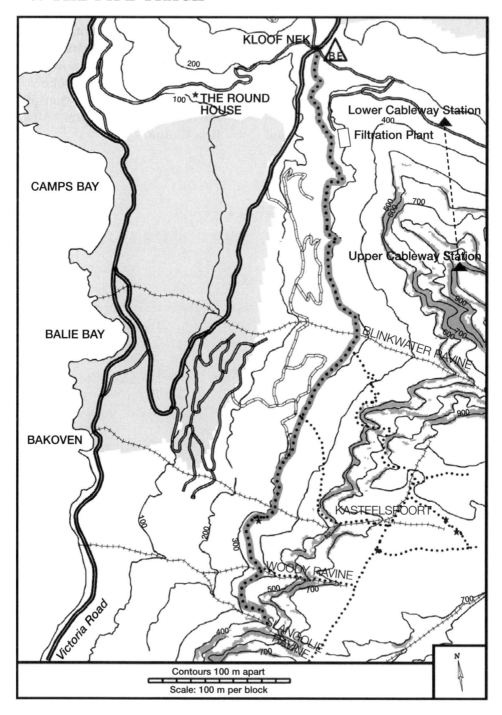

KLOOF NEK

B.E.

200

100 ★ THE ROUND HOUSE

Lower Cableway Station

400

Filtration Plant

CAMPS BAY

500
600
700

Upper Cableway Station

BALIE BAY

BLINKWATER RAVINE

900

900 700

BAKOVEN

900

100

200

KASTEELSPOORT

300

WOODY RAVINE

500 700

700

Victoria Road

400

SLANGOLIE RAVINE

700

700

N

Contours 100 m apart

Scale: 100 m per block

THE PIPE TRACK

CAMPS BAY

Time: 3 hours

Distance: 10 km

Route: Return

Dogs allowed

Brief Description

This is one of the best-known hikes in Cape Town, and certainly one of the oldest, for the Pipe Track was constructed in 1887 to lay the pipeline from the proposed reservoirs on Table Mountain to Kloof Nek. Work began in the same year on the Woodhead Tunnel, to which the track leads. It is a pleasant stroll, mostly along the level, offering wonderful views of the Atlantic Coastline and the Twelve Apostles. In summertime it is recommended that you start in the early morning, when most of the walk is still in shade. It will take 1½ hours to get to where the Pipe Track ends and slightly less time to get back.

Start

At Kloof Nek, on the steps next to the fire hazard board.

Directions

Follow the steps up and at the top you will get a first look at the pipe where it crosses a small ravine. This first section of pipe is known as the Blockhouse Aqueduct (see Points of Interest). The second aqueduct is appropriately named Granite Aqueduct. Discourage your children (and some adults) from trying to do a tightrope act on the pipe. It could spoil your entire day.

Ten to fifteen minutes after starting, you will find yourself below the Kloof Nek Water Treatment Plant (see Points of Interest). Beyond this large building, the Pipe Track plunges down into Diep Sloot, giving you some work to do climbing out the other side.

Every so often you will come across a small brick-and-cement housing containing a valve. They are numbered. At "Air Valve 7" (about 25 minutes after leaving Kloof Nek) look up at the upper cable station, an imposing structure originally built in 1929 and rebuilt in 1997. The big gap on the right is Blinkwater Ravine. At

37

"Air Valve 12" look up and see the deep cut immediately to the right of the cable station. This is Fountain Ravine. Imagine that the Cape Town Municipality contemplated routeing a funicular railway up there, before the cableway method was finally settled on.

Blinkwater Ravine can be considered the halfway point, as it will be reached in 40-45 minutes. Due to a major rockfall it was closed to the public some years ago. Ten minutes further on will bring you to a signpost indicating an important and popular route up the mountain to the Back Table and the reservoirs, namely Kasteelspoort (meaning Castle's Gateway). Keep on the level and five minutes later a jeep track joins your path from the right-hand quarter. This is a relic from the construction of the Apostles Tunnel in 1964.

Beyond "Air Valve 17" look past the three pine tree stumps ahead and pick out a straight scar going directly up the mountain for about 100 m. This leads to the outlet of Apostles Tunnel, which replaced Woodhead Tunnel in 1964.

About one hour after starting you should cross a concrete weir which in winter, after rain, might require some careful footwork. After the weir the gravel path ascends gently, and on the hilltop opposite a forest of invasive spider gums is a solidly built pumphouse, looking more like a mausoleum. Five minutes on will bring you to the base of Woody Ravine: a steep, narrow route to the top. A further five minutes will take you around the corner into Slangolie Ravine. "Dangerous Ascent" notices should inhibit you from going any further than the riverbed.

Perhaps returning the same way doesn't appeal to you, but somehow it is different. Anyway, you should be able to do it in about 15 minutes less than the outward journey.

Points of Interest
❖ The Blockhouse Aqueduct (the first section of pipe you come to) is named after a long since demolished blockhouse and gun battery built in 1781 by the French. A little-known fact is that the French occupied the Cape for about 18 months to protect the Dutch settlers against possible invasion by the English.
❖ The imposing water treatment plant was built in 1938 to treat the water from Woodhead Reservoir. It gave Cape Town its first crystal-clear water. Prior to 1938 the water that came from Cape Town taps was brown. Looking up at the filtration plant, notice the cannon, probably a relic from the French flirtation.

MACLEAR'S BEACON

8

TABLE TOP

Time: 1 hour 45 minutes

Distance: 5,3 km

Route: Circular

Dogs not allowed in cable car

Brief Description

A scenic walk along the table top, from one end to the other and back again. Starting from the upper cable station, the walk crosses the Western Table in just 10 minutes, before dipping down into the "nick" in the table (the top of Platteklip Gorge). A brief climb up onto the Central Table follows the "back" edge of the table with wonderful views over the Table Mountain reservoirs and the southern Peninsula. The return journey from Maclear's Beacon, mostly along the "front" edge of the table, presents some breathtaking vistas of the city and beyond. There are very few places in the world with scenery like this.

The table top is not as flat as it appears from below, and suitable hiking boots are essential, as the path is rough in places. Beware of sudden mist or cloud which in a southeast wind often covers the table top and nothing else, to form the famous tablecloth. Walking in the tablecloth is something akin to staggering around in a dark room and not being able to find any walls, let alone the door.

At places, on the return journey, the path passes very close to the edge. It is no more difficult than walking on a pavement. However, it needs to be borne in mind that the gutter is a very long way down, so be careful not to step off the pavement in a brief moment of chivalry. If you have a serious fear of heights, perhaps you had best give this one a miss.

Start

Catch the cable car ride up the mountain and start from the upper cable station.

Directions

On leaving the upper cable station building, turn sharp left and follow the brown concrete path along the front face of the moun-

8. MACLEAR'S BEACON

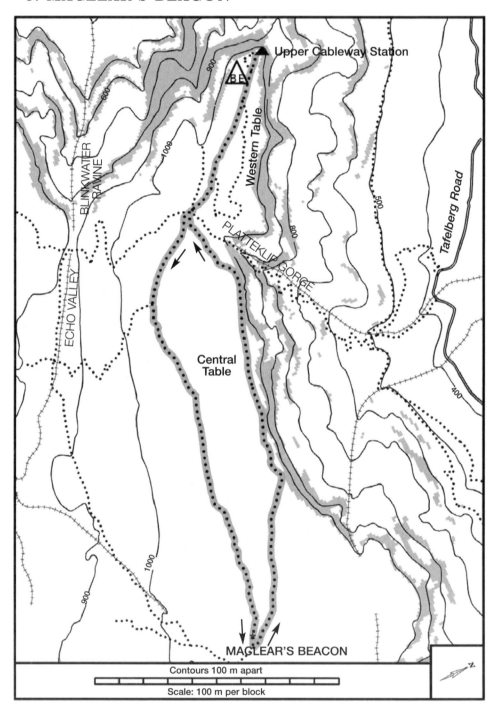

Upper Cableway Station

BE

Western Table

BLINKWATER RAVINE

ECHO VALLEY

PLATTEKLIP GORGE

Central
Table

Tafelberg Road

MACLEAR'S BEACON

Contours 100 m apart

Scale: 100 m per block

tain. After passing a couple of observation platforms it suddenly swings away from the cliff face.

This leads to a large relief map of the Peninsula on a pedestal. From here, keep to the path on the back edge of the Table Top to Platteklip Gorge (the "nick" in the profile of Table Mountain). At a metal pole pointing to Maclear's Beacon take the right-hand path down into the "nick". At the top of Platteklip Gorge is another sign pointing in three directions. Take the path up just to the right of a concrete beacon with marble name plates. For the rest of your walk follow the yellow and white footprints painted on the rocks. Just one minute after starting your climb out of Platteklip, ignore a footprint showing a path to the left. This is your return route. Keep to the clear broad concrete footpath.

Soon you will see the pyramid-shaped Maclear's Beacon in the distance, on your half left.

Seven or eight minutes after leaving the three-way signpost you will come to another. Carry straight on towards Maclear's Beacon. The path now becomes narrower and rougher, and ten minutes later, after passing through some swampy area over boardwalks, it delivers you to Maclear's Beacon.

To return, you need to get to a flat area six or eight metres below the level of the beacon on the Table Bay side. To do this, continue some 50 m beyond the beacon to another signpost. Follow the painted footprints on the only path not indicated by the signpost. Once on the level ground below, turn left and follow the footprints. The path passes a large plaque on the rock face directly below Maclear's Beacon, praising Jan Christiaan Smuts (1870-1950).

About 15 minutes after leaving Maclear's Beacon you will suddenly reach the edge and gaze down on the city far below, and wonder if there can be many more views like this on earth.

The path then clings precariously to the edge for another 10 minutes, before turning inwards to rejoin the outbound path just before Platteklip Gorge. Then simply retrace your steps to the upper cable station.

Points of Interest

✿ Maclear's Beacon at a height of 1 086 m (19 m higher than the cable station end) is the highest point in the Cape Peninsula. It was built in 1844 by Sir Thomas Maclear (1794 - 1879), an important surveyor and astronomer in the early days of the Cape Colony.

9. ECHO VALLEY

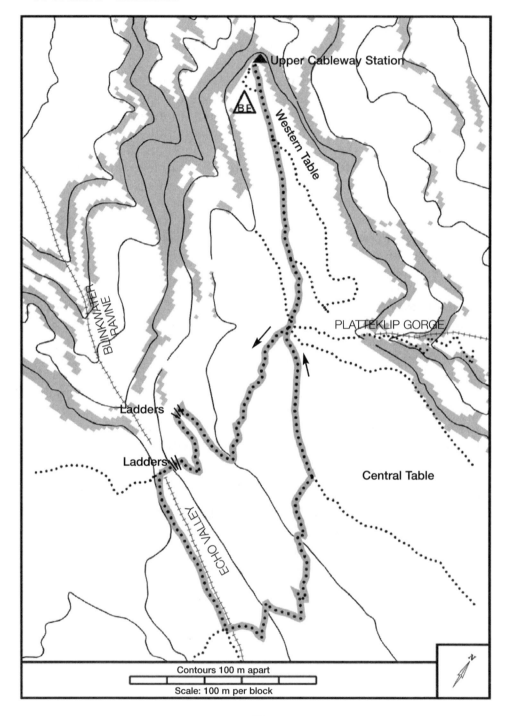

Upper Cableway Station

Western Table

BP

BLINKWATER RAVINE

PLATTEKLIP GORGE

Ladders

Ladders

Central Table

ECHO VALLEY

Contours 100 m apart

Scale: 100 m per block

ECHO VALLEY

TABLE TOP

Time: 2 hours

Distance: 4 km

Route: Circular

Dogs not allowed in cable car

Brief Description

The Front Table is the well-known profile of Table Mountain. Behind it and about 300 m lower in altitude is the Back Table, housing the five main reservoirs of Table Mountain. Separating the Back and Front Tables is the deep Echo Valley. The path down into Echo Valley is well constructed and in places travels over wooden boardwalks, to protect the vegetation. There are three ladders to negotiate on the way down but they are very firmly attached to the rock face and are no cause for concern. The ladders vary in length between 10 and 20 rungs. Then walk the length of the valley in about 10 minutes. The only strenuous part of this walk is getting out of it back up to the table top. This will take about half an hour for reasonably fit hikers.

Start

Catch the cable car ride up the mountain and start the walk from the Upper Cable Station.

Directions

On leaving the upper cable station, turn sharp left and follow the brown concrete path along the front face of the mountain. After passing a couple of observation platforms, it suddenly swings away from the cliff face.

This leads to a large relief map of the Peninsula on a pedestal. From here, keep to the path on the back edge of the Table Top as far as a clear fork in the path, marked by a metal pole. Obey the sign which points to the right, indicating Maclear's Beacon. This is not your destination, but after a steep climb down into the gap in the profile of Table Mountain (the top of Platteklip Gorge) you will soon come to another signpost.

This is one of those mysteries of life which has three pointers at a confluence of four paths. The direction from which you have come is indicated as "Cableway", to the left is "Platteklip Gorge", straight ahead and up is "Maclear's Beacon", and the path to your right, being the most obvious of the lot, is unlabled. Take it. It will lead you to Echo Valley.

Soon Hout Bay's harbour and Sentinel mountain pop into view, as you look down the length of the Twelve Apostles. The route then skirts around to the left and looks down into Blinkwater Ravine, at the head of Echo Valley, and Camps Bay, way below.

Shortly after you catch sight of the Hely-Hutchinson Reservoir on the Back Table, the rocky path drops down and doubles back on itself, about seven minutes after leaving the top of Platteklip. It then drops down the slope into Echo Valley using a series of boardwalks and three ladders. Don't miss the ladders. The first one is just to the left of a sign warning you to use them at your own risk.

Once on the floor of the valley, at its western end you will reach another signpost and four-way crosspaths. Don't attempt to go down Blinkwater Ravine. It has a fatal attraction, with lots of bad history, so rather turn left and walk down the length of the valley to the next signpost, some seven

or eight minutes away.

Please suppress any urge to add to the noise pollution by testing the appropriateness of Echo Valley's name. This auditory version of a Narcissus complex never fails to irritate me!

The next signpost at the eastern end of the valley is in the centre of a four-way boardwalk. Again there are only three direction signs. Again take the unsignposted path up the slope to the left. The others are to Blinkwater Ravine (behind you), Kasteelspoort (to the right) and Maclear's Beacon (straight on). Go across the stream and begin the 30 minutes' slow slog out of Echo Valley. About halfway up, avoid taking a route through a wet marshy area and keep well to the left of it, up the rocky slope.

At the top you will come to another three-way signpost. Surprisingly perhaps, this time there *are* three ways. Turn left toward Platteklip Gorge and return to the Upper Cable Station.

Points of Interest
❀ The Table Mountain Cableway was officially opened on 4 October 1929 and at the time of its rebuilding and enlargement in 1997, had carried close to 9 million passengers without a single mishap. I once told this to a Welsh visitor

friend standing in the queue, and it had the unfortunate effect of making him get back into my car. He wasn't going to tempt fate, and that was that. There was nothing I could do to get him into the cable car.

♣ The cable is visually inspected and lubricated once a month, and once every six months an electromagnetic rope test is done. Had the Cape Town City Council carried out their plans before World War 1, a funicular railway would have been built up Fountain Ravine.

10. NEWLANDS FOREST – WOODCUTTER'S TRAIL

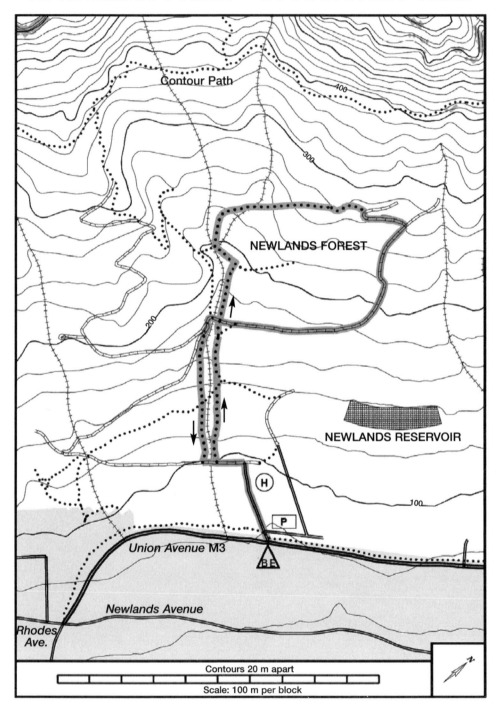

Contour Path

400

300

NEWLANDS FOREST

200

NEWLANDS RESERVOIR

100

(H)

(P)

Union Avenue M3

B B

Newlands Avenue

Rhodes
Ave.

Contours 20 m apart

Scale: 100 m per block

NEWLANDS FOREST – WOODCUTTER'S TRAIL

10

Time: 1 hour 30 minutes

Distance: 3,1 km

Route: Circular

Dogs allowed

Brief Description

Newlands Forest is a maze of unmarked and unmapped paths, which makes it difficult to describe a route accurately. Your chances, therefore, of losing your way in this badly signposted forest are fairly high. But don't let that bother you. There is always the knowledge that your car is at the bottom of the slope, so you can never get seriously lost. Just enjoy the ramble.

The route is almost entirely in shade and a large part of it is along the banks of Newlands Stream. A fine walk for any time of the year and particularly on a hot summer's day, when it is too hot to walk in the open. The Woodcutter's Trail seems to have a number of variations, depending on whom you speak to. This is mine.

Start

From the parking area next to the main gates of Newlands Forest on Union Avenue.

Directions

Pass through the gates and carry straight on ahead for about 200 m to a T-junction and Newlands Forest sign. Turn left and walk for another 150 m along the tarred road until just before a stream and road bridge. Five metres before this bridge, leave the road on a footpath up to the right. Within a few minutes you will come to a sturdy footbridge crossing the stream. At the footbridge turn right for 25 m, then left before reaching a bench. Remember you need to keep following the stream. A few minutes later will bring you to a large metal water pipe crossing the path. Step over the pipe (ignoring the path to the right) and a short distance further up the stream you will come to a gravel road bridge crossing over it.

The path continues following the right-hand side of the stream from the other side of the road.

You will soon come to a T-junction not shown on any maps I've seen. Turn left to head back to the river over wooden walkways. Aim to follow the stream as high up as the path will allow, whilst not crossing it. (Ignore a sign to "Contour Path" painted on a rock.) Soon it will insist on taking you away from the river. The path then breaks out into the open, before plunging back into the forest.

Follow the path away from the stream, to the right over more wooden walkways, before crossing another stream about five minutes later. Here you leave the indigenous forest behind you and pass into a pine plantation. (Busy being felled, at the time of writing.) The path will soon spill onto a gravel road. Follow it down to a T-junction in the road about five minutes after crossing the stream. Now turn down to the right. Head back towards the stream on a well-worn gravel road before reaching the road bridge you passed on the way up Newlands Stream. This is a good spot for a tea break.

When rested, cross over the bridge to the other side of the stream. Walk 50 m up the gravel road before turning left at a fork. Just 25 m down this left fork, turn left again down a path which will take you back to the river bank – this time on the opposite side to when you came up. Follow it all the way back to the tarred road below and then retrace your steps to the entrance.

Notice how badly the river banks have been eroded. The main culprits her are pines and the resultant lack of indigenous vegetation to bind the soil.

Points of Interest

❀ Newlands Forest is the remains of a *buitepost* (outpost) of the Dutch East India Company. It was one of a number in the colony set up to provide timber for housing and ship repairs. This one was known as Paradijs (Paradise), some say due to its close proximity to the fleshpots of Wijnberg and the Tap House at Driekoppen, the site of which is now occupied by a UCT residence.

❀ The main vegetation in the forest is alien blue gums, pines and oak trees, presently being addressed. However, a fair bit of indigenous vegetation remains, with a fairly high population of wild peach (*Kiggelaria africana*). This tree plays host in summertime to armies of black caterpillars which, after pupating, become the common black-and-orange butterfly seen in all Cape gardens. It seems to depend entirely on this particular tree to complete its life cycle.

NEWLANDS FOREST – A TASTE OF PARADISE

11

Time: 1 hour

Distance: 2,6 km

Route: Circular

Dogs allowed

Brief Description

Explore the lower reaches of New-lands Forest and some ruins erro-neously known as Lady Anne Bar-nard's cottage, along mostly level ground in shade. Pleasant views with a dash of history.

Start

From the parking area next to the main gates of Newlands Forest, on Union Avenue.

Directions

Pass through the gates and carry on straight ahead for about 200 m to a T-junction and Newlands Forest sign. Turn left. After approxi-mately 350 m you will run out of tar and come to a boom across the road. Go past the boom and after 150 m on gravel road you will come to an open space and some old ruins on the left. Take the path leading off the far southern cor-ner of the clearing (to the sharp right of an old cement pigpen).

After 100 m down this path, keep right at a fork. Soon you will cross over a cobbled riverbed and 100 m on, bear half left at the edge of a pine forest. (There is a programme afoot to rid Newlands Forest of alien pines, oaks and gums, so any mention of these could be mis-leading. If all else fails, look for stumps!) Emerge from the other side of the pines above some houses and you will be surprised at how high you are, with sweep-ing views of Wynberg Hill. Carry on along the level until you even-tually cross another stream. Fifty metres on the path turns up to the right at the boundary fence of a housing estate and leads into a stand of exceptionally tall blue gums. Just 20 m into the blue gums there is a clear path off to the right which recrosses the stream you crossed lower down. Soon you will come to the ruins of a cluster of buildings built nearly 300 years ago (see Points of Interest).

11. NEWLANDS FOREST – A TASTE OF PARADISE

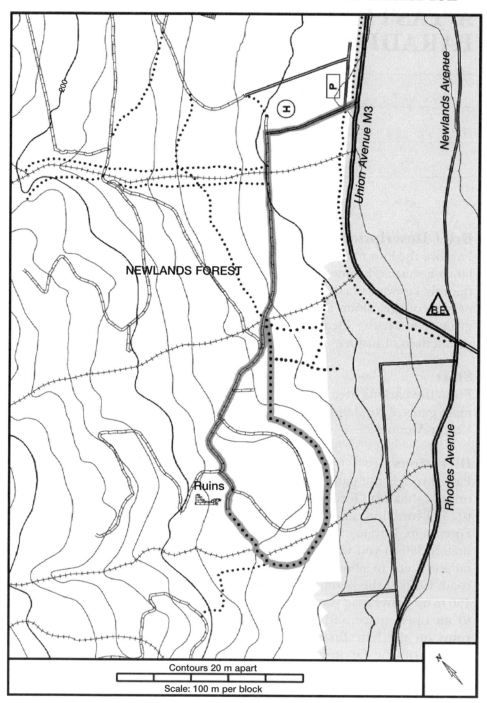

Contours 20 m apart

Scale: 100 m per block

Just past the main building, take the road to the right, then 30 m on, left at the T. At the top of a short hill you will come to a welcome bench. Turn downhill here, down to the right, then left at a second bench and left again at a third bench. A concrete bridge takes you over a river, and then the road forks to the right, bringing you back to the open clearing with the pigpen. From here retrace your steps to the entrance.

Points of Interest

❀ This area was known as Paradijs (Paradise) and was a *buitepost* (outpost) of the Dutch East India Company. (See page 96 on another outpost called De Hel.) The ruins are the remains of the Master Woodcutter's house, built in the early 1700s. He was responsible for protecting the timber resources of Table Mountain. Apart from his own family and a slave, a small garrison of soldiers also lived here, and mounted armed patrols of the forest.

❀ Life for these enlisted men in Paradise was far from heavenly. They suffered poor pay, poor rations and brutal discipline. But for many who enlisted for service in Amsterdam, the alternative was starvation in the economically depressed cities and countryside of Europe.

❀ In the late 1790s, with the Cape under British rule, the house was used briefly by Lady Anne Barnard and her husband Andrew, the Deputy Colonial Secretary. Because of her descriptions of Paradijs in her diary the site became known, rather inappropriately, as Lady Anne Barnard's cottage.

12. NEWLANDS FOREST TO KIRSTENBOSCH

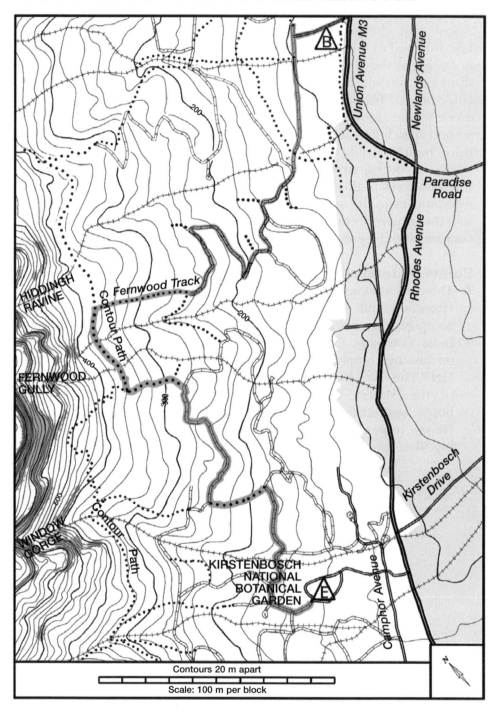

Contours 20 m apart

Scale: 100 m per block

NEWLANDS FOREST TO KIRSTENBOSCH

Jan '05 Mainly part of hibscd → Rhodes

Time: 2 hours

Distance: 6 km

Route: One-way

Dogs allowed on a leash

Brief Description

A steady climb up the slopes of Newlands Forest for less than an hour, mostly on gravel road, to the Contour Path. Then an easy stroll on the level before plunging down to Kirstenbosch down seemingly a million log steps. At Kirstenbosch National Botanical Garden there is a pleasant outdoor restaurant which will lay on a fine champagne breakfast, if this should appeal to you. You will need a second car at the end. The walk is almost entirely in shade.

Start

From the parking area next to the main gates of Newlands Forest, on Union Avenue.

Directions

Pass through the gates and carry on straight ahead for about 200 m to a T-junction and Newlands Forest sign. Turn left. After approximately 350 m you will run out of tar and come to a boom across the road. Go past the boom and after 150 m on gravel road you will come to an open space and some old ruins on the left. Ignore the broad path opposite which goes up obliquely and back to the right. Rather continue a further 75 m on the gravel road to where it is concreted on a sharp corner to the right. Again ignore the right turn at the concrete corner and continue straight on. Cross over a concrete bridge and 30 m further you will come to a fork with a bench on the left. Keep right here. Then right again at the next fork with a bench and right yet again at a third bench.

You are now on the quaintly named Skelmkoppad ("Rogue's Hill Road"). Remain on the broad jeep track for 20 minutes after passing the third bench, ignoring any lesser tracks leading off it. The road finally widens out and comes to an abrupt end.

A narrow path continues towards the mountain and soon points in the direction of Devil's Peak, before becoming more well defined. You are now on the Fernwood Track, as confirmed by its neatly built wooden walkways.

Enjoy a very pleasant upward stroll through the forest at its best, with mottled shade and twittering birds everywhere. About 20 minutes on the Fernwood Track will bring you to a T-junction, which is the Contour Path. Turn left at the T. Ten minutes along the level but rocky Contour Path brings you to the Kirstenbosch boundary, marked by a large signpost. Twenty metres beyond the sign are two huge boulders to the left of the path. Turn down here, following another sign pointing to Kirstenbosch and Silvertree Trail. The log steps up to the right are a continuation of the Contour Path (which now belies its name) and continues all the way to Constantia Nek.

Your route descends rapidly down log steps to a T-junction at a gravel road. Turn right and from here on simply continue to follow the signposts at every intersection to "Garden".

Along the way you will begin to appreciate the vastness of the gardens and the splendid views of Wynberg Hill with its opulent mansions. The restaurant awaits you below with a champagne break-fast. It is hoped you have brought the right set of keys for the return journey!

Points of Interest

❁ Kirstenbosch is a treasure trove of indigenous South African plants; more than 6 000 of them in fact, making this one of the world's largest and most important botanical gardens.

❁ It was originally called Leendertsbos, after Van Riebeeck appointed one Leendert Cornelissen to be in charge of a woodcutters' station there. It kept this name until the late 1700s, when the Kirsten family began farming in the area. The farm then passed through various hands until it was bought in 1895 by Cecil John Rhodes for the princely sum of 9 000 pounds. On his death in 1902 he left it in a trust for the people of South Africa. However, it was another 11 years before an Act of Parliament officially declared Kirstenbosch a national botanical garden.

❁ One of Kirstenbosch's most well-known and delightful landmarks is a fraud – or at best a shaky urban legend. Ever since childhood Lady Anne Barnard's bath has conjured up for me an image of a beautiful aristocratic lady bathing in this crystal pool, surrounded by verdant ferns and the sound of birdsong. It came as a rude surprise that she never even clapped eyes on this captivating pool. It was built in 1811, fully nine years after she left the colony. The pool is referred to, more correctly, as the Bird Bath, for not only is it built in the shape of a bird, it was built by Colonel Christopher Bird on the property which had been leased to him during his official term of office as Deputy Colonial Secretary. Lady Anne would not have enjoyed too much privacy here today, for Kirstenbosch is receiving half a million visitors a year. If she had had an open bath anywhere it would have been in Paradijs, in what is today known as Newlands Forest. Try to visit this lovely pool and visual pun in the centre of the gardens, before being lured away by the smell of bacon and eggs coming from the restaurant.

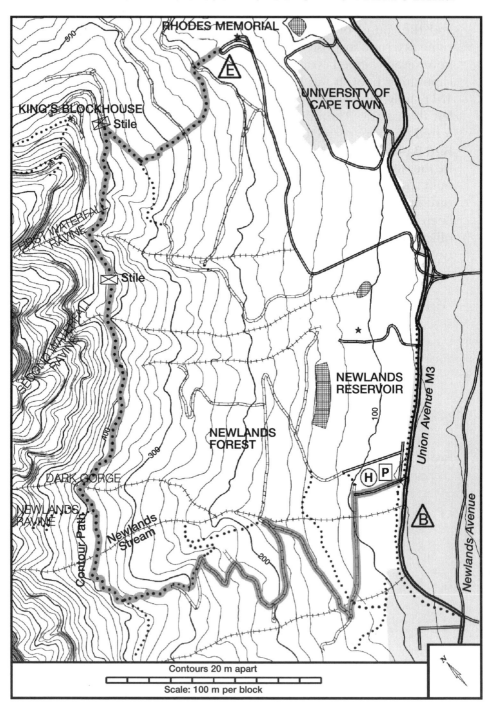

RHODES MEMORIAL

UNIVERSITY OF CAPE TOWN

KING'S BLOCKHOUSE

Stile

Stile

NEWLANDS RESERVOIR

NEWLANDS FOREST

Union Avenue M3

DARK GORGE

NEWLANDS RAVINE

Newlands Stream

Contour Path

Newlands Avenue

Contours 20 m apart

Scale: 100 m per block

NEWLANDS FOREST TO RHODES MEMORIAL

For '05 but started at Kilburd

13

Time: 2 hours 30 minutes

Distance: 6,4 km

Route: One-way

Dogs allowed

Brief Description

A steady climb up the slopes of Newlands Forest for less than an hour, mostly on gravel road, to the Contour Path. Then an easy stroll along the level through dense and mostly indigenous forest, before descending to Rhodes Memorial where there is a tea room to quench your thirst. You will need a second car at the end. The walk is almost entirely in shade.

Start

From the parking area next to the main gates of Newlands Forest, on Union Avenue.

Directions

Pass through the gates and carry on straight ahead for about 200 m to a T-junction and Newlands Forest sign. Turn left. After approximately 350 m you will run out of tar and come to a boom across the road. Go past the boom and after 150 m on gravel road you will come to an open space and some old ruins on the left. Ignore the broad path opposite which goes up obliquely and back to the right. Rather continue a further 75 m on the gravel road to where it is concreted on a sharp corner to the right. Now take the right turn and ignore the road carrying straight on at the bend.

The road climbs steadily on its way up through a pine plantation (soon to be cut down). Where it meets a stand of gum trees (*Eucalyptus* spp,) (also on the executioner's list) it joins another road. Turn left here and continue the upward climb on the road, ignoring a sign inviting you to leave the road on a short cut to the Contour Path. Keep right at the next bend when tempted to go down a side road, and ten minutes later follow a sign indicating "Contour Path". This is another short-cut path, but if you were to stay on the road you

57

would finish at the same place anyway.

When the road eventually runs out you will be confronted by some steep log steps, but the Contour Path, and the end of your upward climb, is only a couple of minutes away. Once on the Contour Path, turn right.

The walk is now at its prettiest as it passes through dense indigenous forest and winds its way in and out of ravines. It remains on the level for another hour if you don't stop. But you might want to do just that at an appropriate spot, for a breather and refreshments. Perhaps Newlands Stream, or the aptly named Dark Gorge?

Towards the end of the Contour Path, on the slopes of Devil's Peak, you will have to climb a ladder over the fence or go through a turnstile. This marks the boundary between Newlands Forest and Groote Schuur Estate – Cecil John Rhodes's gift to South Africa – which included the University of Cape Town. Your walk through the estate will take another 20 minutes before you come to another turnstile and ladder, marking the opposite bound-ary. Just before the second stile, take a sharp right turn and double back to take the path down to Rhodes Memorial. Avoid the first couple of short cuts and take the third turnoff to the left, along this descending path. The descent from Contour Path to Rhodes Memorial will take 20-25 minutes.

Points of Interest

❀ Rhodes died in 1902 and 10 years later, on his birthday, 5 July 1912, this memorial was officially opened at one of his favourite viewpoints. It was designed by Sir Herbert Baker and funded by public contributions. But Rhodes's real memorial is perhaps the University of Cape Town, for he donated the land on which it stands today. Appropriately, any letters posted at UCT's post office are franked "Rhodes Gift".

❀ Another proposal after his death was to place a 50-storey high "Colossus of Rhodes" statue, perched on top of Lion's Head. Thank heavens we finished up with this lesser edifice on the slopes of Devil's Peak.

LIESBEEK RIVER TRAIL   14

Time: 45 minutes

Distance: 3 km

Route: One-way

Dogs allowed

Brief Description

The Liesbeek River, birthplace of the South African economy, runs through the history of the Cape like a silver thread. It is possible to walk alongside or very close to the river all the way from Kirstenbosch to Observatory. But near each end it is necessary to walk along tarred roads, which is not quite on, in terms of the nature of this book. So we shall confine ourselves to the middle section, which sticks almost exclusively to a constructed footpath alongside the banks of the river. This will also ensure that you end conveniently at a most pleasant venue in a tranquil setting, where one can have a light meal and a beer or three. You can catch a train back to Rosebank station. The route is wheelchair-friendly. Guided walks can be booked for the upper section only, by phoning (021) 686-4939.

Start

From Mowbray railway station, drive down Durban Road to the Liesbeek Parkway and turn right. Six hundred and fifty metres along, at the next traffic lights, where Alma Road crosses Liesbeek Parkway, find a place to park in Alma Road. Your starting point is at the corner of Alma and Liesbeek, on the mountain side of the freeway. Rosebank station is close to the end of Alma Road.

Directions

Walk along the pavement of Liesbeek Parkway southwards for about 100 paces to the road bridge crossing the river. Just beyond the bridge turn right onto a gravel track, which will take you down to the river. About 100 m down the track is a wooden footbridge. Do *not* cross here, but continue on up the left bank until you reach a concrete bridge. Cross over the river here and almost

59

14. LIESBEEK RIVER TRAIL

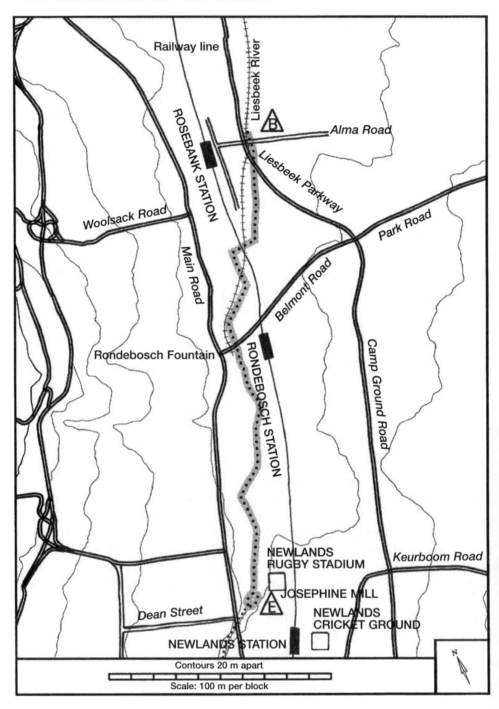

Railway line

Liesbeek River

Alma Road

ROSEBANK STATION

Liesbeek Parkway

Woolsack Road

Park Road

Main Road

Belmont Road

Rondebosch Fountain

RONDEBOSCH STATION

Camp Ground Road

NEWLANDS
RUGBY STADIUM

Keurboom Road

JOSEPHINE MILL

Dean Street

NEWLANDS
CRICKET GROUND

NEWLANDS STATION

Contours 20 m apart

Scale: 100 m per block

immediately you will be forced under the railway lines. Once out of the subway, turn sharp left and follow the railway line for 150 m as far as a metal fence which appears to block your way. But it doesn't. There is a narrow escape to the right, and now you're back alongside the river. Keep to its left bank to where the river goes under Belmont Road, near Rondebosch Fountain (see Points of Interest). Just beyond the fountain is St. Paul's Church, the minister of which was allowed in terms of an old Cape law to raise his cows on the Rondebosch Common. It seems almost a pity that the present-day minister doesn't have any cows.

Cross over Belmont Road and keep to the left bank (unless you want to pop into Riverside Shopping Mall). Either side meets at a concrete bridge. Keep to the left bank and a minute or two later cross over another (this time wooden) bridge. This is known as the Telkom Bridge (the cost of which was paid by Telkom). Then the route takes you through a little park before crossing over yet another wooden bridge to get back to the left bank. Here the path is built out over the canal to accommodate an old tennis court. Now cross over Rouwkoop Road to continue along the left bank. Three minutes later, cross over one of the original bridges at the old pumphouse, which a few years ago was a pub called Whistlers. This section of the trail is known as the Albion Springs Development and the pathway is thanks to the developer's generosity. Weirs have been introduced to oxygenate the water, as well as concrete circles cut into the floor of the canal and filled with stones to give refuge to aquatic animals, particularly in times of flood. Notice the granite block seats along this section, making a serious statement to vandals.

Kingfishers, sacred ibis and black duck are sometimes seen on this part of the river.

Cross over an access route to Newlands Rugby Ground, and you will be walking along a path sponsored by Southern Life. This will lead you to opposite Josephine Mill, where you will be able to end your journey in pleasant surroundings. Read the plaque opposite the mill and then continue to a point where you can turn left and come back along the opposite bank to Threshers Tea Garden – part of Cape Town's only surviving and operational water mill. There is also a milling museum, blacksmithing exhibit and conference centre on the premises. You can watch a milling demonstration and buy stone-ground flour and other by-products. It is hoped you have someone here to pick you up and return you to your car at the start, or simply catch the train back to Rosebank station.

Points of Interest

❀ The *Friends of the Liesbeek* is a society keen to introduce you to its flowers, birds and trees – and the story of our rainbow nation; for its birth cries were first heard on the banks of this river. They organize regular guided hikes down the entire river course. This is truly the country's most historic river, so phone them to book a guided trail from Kirstenbosch to the Josephine Mill on (021) 686-4939. You don't need a booking to do that section of the trail, but you will learn a great deal more if you do. The section described here is not guided.

❀ *Lies* means reeds and *beek* refers to a stream; so the Liesbeek River is one of those linguistic repetitions. Clearly the National Place Names Committee wasn't paying attention at the time. Anyway, now that it's mostly canalized, reeds can only be seen in the lower reaches.

❀ Rondebosch Fountain: On or near this spot stood a clump of thorn trees which gave Rondebosch its original name – *'t Ronde Doornbosjen*. The foun-

tain, one of Cape Town's two remaining street horse troughs, was donated by George Pigot Moodie in 1891. This colourful character, a Transvaal mining pioneer and later Surveyor General of the Transvaal, lived for part of each year in Rondebosch at Westbrook, now Genadendal, the State President's Residence. He ran an electric cable to the fountain from Westbrook to light the fountain at night, thus providing the first suburban electric light in the country.

❀ The Josephine Mill: Jacob Letterstedt, a Swede who came to the Cape as an 1820 settler, built this mill in 1840 and named it after Crown Princess Josephine of his native Sweden. His prosperous and diversified business activities included milling and brewing.

❀ The Breweries: You will know your walk is near its end from the strong smell of hops. No fewer than seven breweries used to operate along the banks of the Liesbeek. Long forgotten breweries such as Mariendahl, Canon, Cloetes and Letterstedt were bought up by one Anders Ohlsson, another Swedish immigrant. Born out of this takeover is the modern-day S.A. Breweries.

YELLOWWOOD TRAIL 15

Jan '05

KIRSTENBOSCH

Time: 1 hour 30 minutes

Distance: 3,2 km

Route: Circular

Dogs not allowed

Brief Description

A well-marked forest trail which winds its way up the densely wooded slopes of Kirstenbosch National Botanical Garden to the Contour Path, then down again through more indigenous forest in which many of the individual trees are nameplated. Almost the entire walk is in shade and is therefore ideal for either summer or winter walking. None of the indigenous trees are deciduous (lose their leaves in winter) so you are assured of a dense canopy all year round. It is moderately strenuous in comparison to many other walks in this book, in so far as there are very few level sections. It is either up or it is down, but nowhere is it excessively steep. Amongst the indigenous trees you can expect to identify are: assegai, bladdernut, Cape beech (boekenhout), Cape chestnut, Cape saffron, hard pear, ironwood, red pear, stinkwood, turkey-berry and wild peach. And of course, yellowwood.

Start

At the far end of the upper (Garden Centre) parking area of Kirstenbosch is a turnstile entrance where you will be required to pay to enter the gardens.

Directions

Go through the turnstiles and follow the signpost indicating the Yellowwood Trail. These well-placed signs will guide you comfortably all the way. Soon go past the tearoom on the right and down some steps. Follow the sign pointing to Smuts's Track at the bottom of the steps. After going over a wooden footbridge, turn right at the junction marked "Smuts Track" and "Yellowwood Trail". This is opposite the interesting Fragrance Garden. Go up the gravel track which takes you past an equally interesting Braille Trail.

63

15. YELLOWWOOD TRAIL

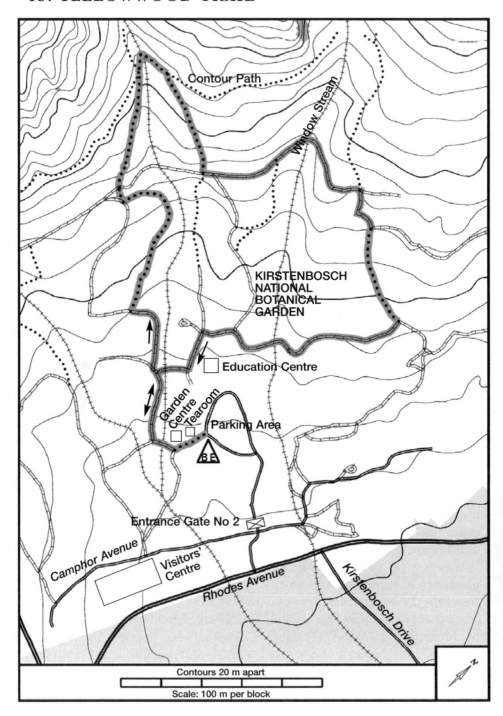

Contour Path

Window Stream

KIRSTENBOSCH
NATIONAL
BOTANICAL
GARDEN

Education Centre

Garden
Centre
Tearoom

Parking Area

BE

Entrance Gate No 2

Camphor Avenue

Visitors'
Centre

Rhodes Avenue

Kirstenbosch Drive

Contours 20 m apart

Scale: 100 m per block

After a short while the gravel track bends to the left. Just after the bend you have a choice of sticking to the original trail, simply by remaining on the road, or taking a short cut up a path marked "Contour Path". This is much more interesting, and rejoins the road further up. After seven to ten minutes up this path you will reach a T-junction of steps just above the road you were originally on. Turn right and go up about 36 steep steps, before crossing over another gravel road.

Follow the Yellowwood Trail signpost and continue the upward climb for a further 10 minutes, before coming to the Contour Path. Once there, notice the plaque on the rock marked "Smuts' Track". You'll certainly want a rest at this, the highest point of your walk. So take a seat on the selfsame rock regularly used for a breather by former world statesman Field Marshal Jan Christiaan Smuts. Once rested in this tranquil setting, go right along the Contour Path, following the Yellowwood Trail sign. A few metres further on will bring you to a stream (which can be a raging torrent after rain). This is the stream which tumbles down Skeleton Gorge, and here it becomes a most spectacular waterfall when the river is flowing strongly.

A minute or two beyond the waterfall, leave the Contour Path and go down some steep steps to the right (again a signpost will guide you). These steps will bring you to a meeting of ways. Your path meets three gravel roads. Follow the sign up the road going half left. Three minutes later you will emerge from the forest to be confronted by the imposing face of Fernwood Buttress, literally towering above you.

A couple of minutes later, cross over a cobbled Window Stream which has a welcome bench next to it, inviting you for a tea break. Follow the notice at the next crossroads down to the right, and a minute later leave the gravel road to go down some log steps. This section is marked by some healthy-looking silver tree saplings (see Points of Interest).

When back on the gravel road again, turn right. The road crosses Window Stream once more, and from here continue following the Yellowwood Trail signs, until you reach a signpost saying "Garden". Follow the signposts marked "Garden" and these will deliver you safely back to your car.

Points of Interest

✿ Silver trees *(Leucadendron argenteum)* are very special for greater Cape Town, for they grow naturally nowhere else in the world except here. Even within this area they are somewhat snobbish about their address. Reasonable-sized stands are confined to only three places: Kirstenbosch, the southern slopes of Lion's Head and the Helderberg Basin around Somerset West. Numerous attempts have been made to cultivate them elsewhere in the world, but they seem to represent your typical Capetonian – they want to live here and nowhere else. Nothing can quite compare with the shimmering and glinting of the leaves in a gentle breeze. But there is a downside. They are very susceptible to root rot and collar rot caused by a fungus (*Phytophthora cinnamomi*). This explains the common sight of an occasional dead tree amongst a group of healthy ones. The mortality rate is particularly high at the seedling stage.

STINKWOOD TRAIL

Time: 45 minutes

Distance: 1,5 km

Route: Circular

Dogs not allowed

Brief Description

Kirstenbosch is blessed with three indigenous forest trails, and this is the easiest and shortest of the three. Of the other two, one is described in the previous chapter, and the Silvertree Trail is too strenuous to be included in this book; it also takes three hours, which gives a good idea of just how large Kirstenbosch really is. The Stinkwood Trail, despite being the shortest, still requires a bit of effort to climb log steps. There is a modest entrance fee and you could end your walk with refreshments in the tearoom.

Start

At the far end of the upper (Garden Centre) parking area of Kirstenbosch through a turnstile entrance.

Directions

Go through the turnstiles and pass the Garden Centre, tearoom and lecture hall on your right, before coming to the amphitheatre steps. Follow the signpost pointing to Smuts' Track and within a few metres, cross over a little stream. Opposite the Fragrance Garden turn right to start up the beginning of Smuts' Track. After this has taken you past the Braille Trail, take the first turn to the right. Use the footbridge if the river is flowing too strongly. Ahead of you will be the tiled roof of the Education Centre. On reaching its perimeter fence, turn left and from here on follow the signposts for the Stinkwood Trail. At the next junction, continue the upward climb, soon coming to some log steps. These will lead you eventually to a forest glade called Donkergat.

Near the top of your climb you will reach an enormous dead pine tree. It has clearly been ringbarked in order to kill it, as it is very much an invasive alien in this indigenous forest. Ringbarking,

16. STINKWOOD TRAIL

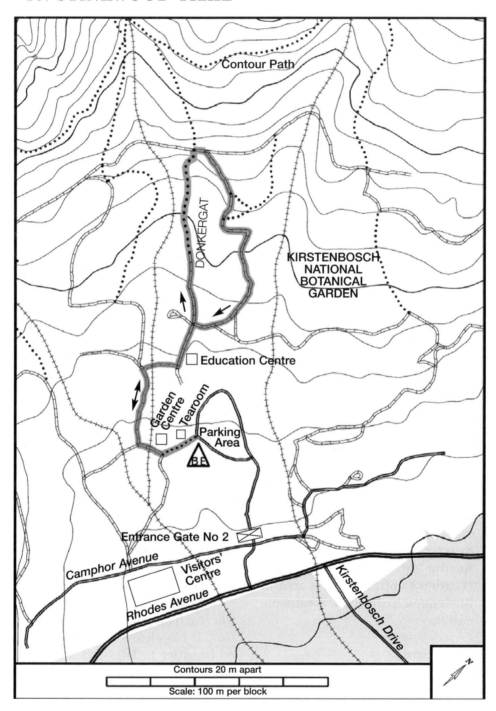

Contour Path

DONKERGAT

KIRSTENBOSCH
NATIONAL
BOTANICAL
GARDEN

☐ Education Centre

Garden
Centre ☐ Tearoom

☐ Parking
Area

B.B.

Entrance Gate No 2

Camphor Avenue

Visitors'
Centre

Rhodes Avenue

Kirstenbosch Drive

Contours 20 m apart

Scale: 100 m per block

or cutting through the bark in a complete ring around the base of a tree, has the same effect as if you were to punch holes in a drinking straw.

One minute's walk after the dead pine will bring you to a gravel road. At the road turn right and right again, following the signpost. However, at the fork a few metres after joining the road, notice a tree with a plastic nameplate on it. The early Dutch settlers had some pretty indelicate names for certain plants, such as the strong-smelling *paardepis*. But this particular nameplate has always rather tickled me. There's nothing unusual about the common turkey-berry tree, except its Afrikaans name: *gewone bokdrol* describes its fallen berries perfectly.

The gravel road now tumbles down the slope rather steeply, ignoring side roads coming in from the left. Eventually you will come to a fork. Keep right in order to meet the path you came up on at a T-junction. Turn left and retrace your steps back to the garden.

Points of Interest

❀ Kirstenbosch (or Kirstenbosch National Botanical Garden, as it is more correctly known) is much more than just one of the world's leading botanical gardens. It is the showcase of the richest floral kingdom on earth.

❀ The globe is divided into six botanical regions or kingdoms. One of these, the Cape Floral Kingdom, stretches along a narrow coastal strip from Clanwilliam in the north to Cape Town and Grahamstown in the east. It is the smallest of the six kingdoms by a long chalk, and yet it is far and away the richest. Representing only 0,04% of the world's land mass, this tiny area boasts about 8 500 different species of flowering plants – many more per square km than its nearest rival. The Scottish Highlanders are so proud to have most of the heather (*Erica* spp.) from the 21 different species in all of Europe. We have more than 650 and keep discovering more.

❀ The plants of the Western Cape are remarkably different from plants found anywhere else in the world, and more than two-thirds of them are found nowhere else – which makes one look at Kirstenbosch with renewed interest.

17. KLAASSENSBOSCH

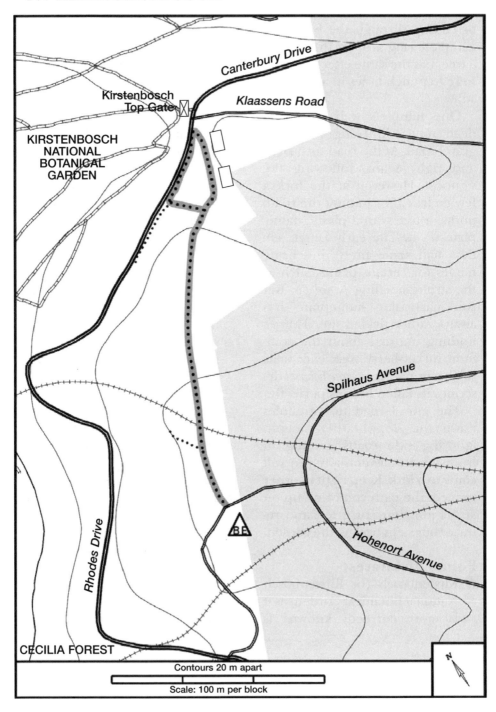

Canterbury Drive

Kirstenbosch
Top Gate

Klaassens Road

KIRSTENBOSCH
NATIONAL
BOTANICAL
GARDEN

Spilhaus Avenue

Rhodes Drive

Hohenort Avenue

CECILIA FOREST

Contours 20 m apart

Scale: 100 m per block

KLAASSENSBOSCH 17

KIRSTENBOSCH

Time: 20 minutes

Distance: 1,1 km

Route: Return

Dogs allowed on leash

Brief Description

This outlying piece of Kirstenbosch Botanical Garden is an enclave of indigenous trees, below Rhodes Drive instead of above it, as one would expect for Kirstenbosch.

If you should ever want to see a microcosm of our indigenous trees, this is where to go. The broad jeep track stretches from Hohenort Avenue to Kirstenbosch's top gate, a distance of a mere 500 m. But in that short stretch you will see silver trees, yellowwoods, wild peach, wild olive, mountain cypress, keurboom, rooiels and many others. Unfortunately, at the time of writing they were not labelled, so *A Leaf Key to 45 Common Trees of Table Mountain* by P A S Wilson would come in quite handy. It should be obtainable from the Kirstenbosch Botanical Society's bookshop.

This walk could be done with your aging grandmother.

Start

On Rhodes Drive, opposite the Cecilia Forest parking area, is Hohenort Avenue. Three hundred metres down Hohenort Avenue you will come to a gate on the left, marking the start of this short walk.

Directions

Enter through the gate and follow the broad jeep track. After 100 metres ignore the fork to the left and continue straight on, and a minute or so later cross over a stream. You probably won't see it in the dense undergrowth but will certainly hear it, babbling its way under the road. This stream has increased considerably in volume in recent years since the removal of blue gums and blackwoods higher up (see Points of Interest).

The track will lead you to a green mesh fence on the right. Ignore the broad track coming

71

down from the left; this is your return route. Walk up alongside the fence admiring the palatial mansions on the other side. At the top of the rise is a gate letting you out of Klaassensbosch to connect across the road with Kirstenbosch proper, through the so-called Top Gate (more correctly known as the Rycroft Gate).

Return by staying inside the fence and following it around to the left, back in the direction from which you have come. The track turns away from the fence at a locked double gate and rejoins the route on which you came up. Now retrace your steps.

Points of Interest

❁ This area was not always as pristine as it is today. From the early 1900s until as recently as 1978 this land was completely overrun by alien gums, pines and blackwoods, planted there for commercial purposes. In the 1980s Kirstenbosch became engaged in a major re-generation process, and gradually removed most of the aliens. These drank enormous amounts of water and totally dried up the stream that you heard happily babbling away.

❁ Over the years the unwelcome aliens have been replaced with the kind co-operation of groups such as the Botanical Society, schools, the Boy Scouts and even the Army, who were persuaded to spread selected seeds and plant saplings. Every year a hack is organized to remove persistent aliens. The results of this amazing transformation are there for all to see. Slowly but surely the natural fauna and bird life are beginning to re-establish themselves.

❁ This is what Cape forests should look like – not the monotonous monospecific pine or blue gum forest across the road in Cecilia Forest. There is a heavy spot fine for allowing dogs off the leash. Mountain bikes are not allowed.

SANDY BAY TO OUDESCHIP

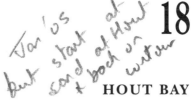

Jan '05 but start at How sand back on water

18

Time: 2 hours 45 minutes

Distance: 6,8 km

Route: Return

Dogs allowed

Brief Description

An interesting and varied walk, even without the nudists. Entirely on the level, this walk starts at the southern end of Llandudno along an extremely well-trodden path, crosses Sandy Bay beach and then dives into the bushes and continues parallel to the coast, until reaching the rocky peninsula of Oudeschip. From here you will see two shipwrecks and learn about a third.

Start

Leaving the coastal road between Camps Bay and Hout Bay, turn down the road to Llandudno. After 600 m you will come to a sharp bend to the right. At this point continue straight along Fisherman's Bend Road. After negotiating six speed bumps, turn right into Sandy Bay Road. Then follow the signposts to Sandy Bay all the way down Sunset Avenue almost to the bottom. On the last

sharp bend there is a parking area, at the end of which begins the path to Sandy Bay.

Directions

The well-worn path to Sandy Bay must have been trodden by hundreds of thousands, if not millions of people over the years since it became famous (or infamous) as a popular nudist beach in the early 1960s. If you have a problem with nudity, or if you're only doing this walk to ogle, then best you stay at home. Neither Mother Grundys nor voyeurs are welcome here.

At the beginning of the walk the broad path passes through coastal fynbos and above Nudist Bay, before becoming a boardwalk for about 80 metres.

When tempted by paths to left and right, just maintain a route more or less parallel to the coast. Ten minutes after starting you will come to a rocky peninsula known

18. SANDY BAY TO OUDESCHIP

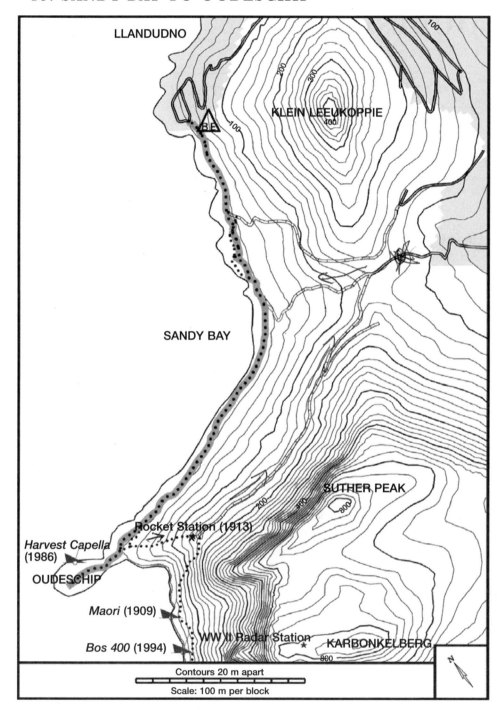

LLANDUDNO

KLEIN LEEUKOPPIE

SANDY BAY

SUTHER PEAK

Rocket Station (1913)

Harvest Capella
(1986)

OUDESCHIP

Maori (1909)

Bos 400 (1994)

WW II Radar Station

KARBONKELBERG

Contours 20 m apart

Scale: 100 m per block

locally as Hammersteen. This marks the spot where Hammer, an old coloured fisherman, was washed off the rocks and drowned. Later generations of fishermen still avoid the area for fear of *Hammer se spook* (Hammer's ghost).

Marlene's Bay lies between Hammersteen and Sandy Bay proper and has a perennial spring, hidden in the bushes at its northern end. This is the only fresh water on this entire stretch of coastline.

Walk the length of Sandy Bay. If it's a hot day on a weekend, you might feel the need to stare blankly at the sand one metre directly ahead of you as you walk. This way, you'll avoid feeling awkward at being overdressed. On the other hand it might be easier to take off all your clothes, and put them on again once you are at the other end of the beach.

The far end of Sandy Bay beach is littered with boulders. Your way is between the boulders and the bush, for about 250 m, before coming to a notice warning you of the dangers of attempting to follow the coastline all the way around Karbonkelberg to Hout Bay. You need not worry about this, as you are not going nearly that far. Should the notice have been taken out by heavy seas or vandals, another nearby landmark is what I have always called Umbrella Rock – a large granite rock

with a milkwood tree growing bravely out of it in the shape of a one-sided umbrella.

The notice – or rock – is the point at which you must leave the rocky shoreline and proceed to about 100 linear metres above the water's edge. The path itself was clear at the time of writing, shortly after a fire. The distance from Sandy Bay beach to the rocky peninsula of Oudeschip is considerably greater than it looks. The path through the bush remains pretty well parallel to the coast all the way. Don't be tempted back down onto the rocks until the very end.

After about twenty to twenty-five minutes from the beach the bush path will take you through a narrow gap between two rocks, and suddenly there is Shorty's Cave, a fairly substantial granite shelter which used to be the home of Shorty and his three sons, a modern-day Strandloper family.

Soon afterwards you will reach the rocky peninsula of Oudeschip. On the other side of it is the deep bay of Leeugat, grave of the *Maori*.

The huge floating crane you see on the other side of Leeugat (definitely no longer floating) is the wreck of the *Bos 400*. And on the right-hand side of the Oudeschip peninsula are the rusty remains of the *Harvest Capella*.

Explore the peninsula, for it has some bizarre and interesting rock formations which are most unusual for granite. Return by the same route and notice how remarkably alike Lion's Head and Little Lion's Head appear to be from this angle and distance.

Do not attempt to reach the wreck of the *Bos 400* from this point. Its distance away is extremely deceptive and the return journey would take all of two and a half hours. Whatever you do, don't be fooled into thinking Hout Bay harbour is just around the corner from the *Bos 400*. It is a six-hour walk which is both exposed and strenuous. Every year it claims its victims from unsuspecting hikers who think Hout Bay is "just around the corner".

Points of Interest

❧ The most obvious of the three shipwrecks in the area of Oudeschip is clearly the *Bos 400*. She came to grief in June 1994 in driving rain and gale-force winds and the 18 crew members were all lifted to safety by helicopter. But imagine the scene 85 years earlier, without the luxury of modern rescue techniques. Just after midnight on 5 August 1909 the British steamship *Maori* struck the rocks just below your vantage point, on the south side of the Oudeschip peninsula. Only 22 of the 53 crewmen lived to tell the tale of what has been described as the most dramatic rescue by rocket apparatus ever carried out on the South African coast. As it had taken 48 hours to transport the rocket apparatus to the rescue scene it was decided in 1913 to build a rocket station to house rescue equipment, in order to avert another disaster. The rocket station still stands at the top of the hill, empty and useless. Helicopters have long since taken the place of firing a line-carrying rocket over a stricken vessel.

❧ The third member of the trio of shipwrecks is the *Harvest Capella*. She was a long-liner owned by Sea Harvest Corporation in Saldanha Bay. These long-liners used to go out fishing for hake on long lines with hooks every few metres, instead of using nets. This way they avoided bruising the fish and could get up to three times the price by flying them fresh to Spain. *Harvest Capella* stopped high-flying rather abruptly in 1986.

ORANGEKLOOF

19

HOUT BAY

Time: 1 to 7 hours

Distance: Varies

Route: Circular

Dogs not allowed

Brief Description

This is a special experience: a wilderness within a city. For three generations there have been stringent fire protection measures to keep the public out of this arboreal version of Jurassic Park. Only since 1996 has it been possible to step back in time and walk through indigenous forest that is essentially the same as it was many centuries ago.

A number of hikes are possible. The main circuit takes three hours along a gently sloping gravel ring road, with shorter guided and self-guided hikes starting from the proposed Environmental Education Centre. This is an educational experience in an outdoor laboratory.

Start

At Constantia Nek from the parking area on the Cape Town side and through the gate at the Hout Bay end.

Directions

Entry is *strictly* by permit only. At the time of writing this edition, Table Mountain National Park had taken over control of Orangekloof, and plans are afoot to open an Environmental Education Centre there. Free permits can be obtained for groups of 12, with guide provided, by phoning (021) 689 4441.

The main circular route is along a gravel road which encircles the entire amphitheatre, crossing no fewer than seven ravines before reaching a high point and returning to base. In clockwise order the ravines have interesting names such as Longkloof, Orangekloof, Black Slab Ravine, Intake Ravine, Frustration Gully, Frustration Gorge and finally, at the top, Disa Gorge. If time allows, try to persuade your guide to take you to Hell's Gates, one of the most beautiful waterfall ravines I have ever seen. It

19. ORANGEKLOOF

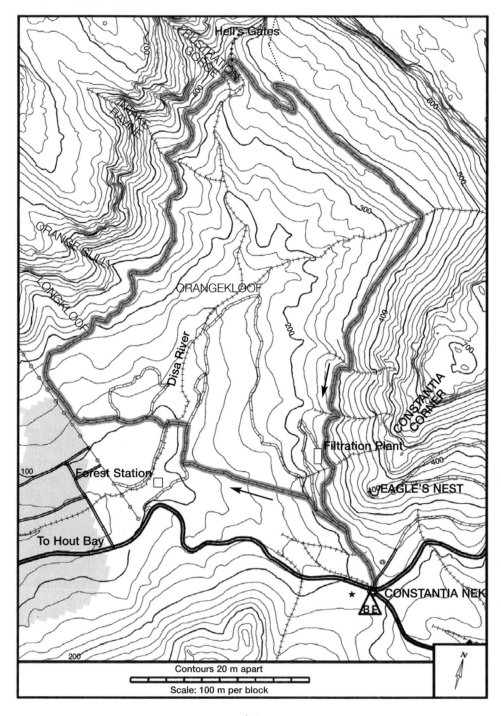

Contours 20 m apart

Scale: 100 m per block

took me half a century to discover this gem on my very own doorstep.

Points of Interest

✿ Not since 1933 has there been a serious fire in the indigenous forests of Orangekloof. This is probably thanks largely to stringent fire protection measures, which severely restricted public access for over 60 years. In 1933 the forest was close to being annihilated. Today it is well on the way to recovery and has expanded considerably since then. Important indigenous species of trees to be found, include silver trees, Cape beech (boekenhout), wild peach, yellowwood, red alder (rooiels), wild olive, assegai, hard pear and milkwood.

20. THE MANGANESE MINE

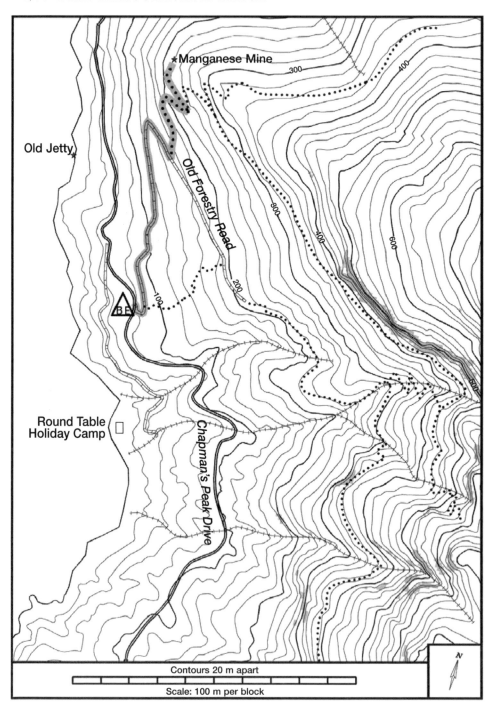

*Manganese Mine

Old Jetty

Old Forestry Road

300

400

800

400

600

500

BE

Round Table
Holiday Camp

Chapman's Peak Drive

200

100

N

Contours 20 m apart

Scale: 100 m per block

THE MANGANESE MINE   20

Brief Description

A climb to about 200 m above sea level with splendid views over Hout Bay and an interesting peek into an abandoned mine shaft with a dash of history. Remember to take a torch.

Start

On Chapman's Peak Drive from the parking area 250 m beyond East Fort, where the gravel forestry road doubles back towards Hout Bay (1,5 km from the Chapman's Peak Hotel).

Directions

Follow the gravel track to the point where it doubles back on itself. About 150 m after the hairpin bend, look for a path going back and up to the left. It is marked by a rocky cairn. A little way along this path you might notice the odd sheet of rusty galvanized iron indicating the last remains of the chutes, which took the ore down to the jetty below. It is important that you count the number of zigzags as the path begins to wind its way up the slope. Immediately after the fourth zigzag you will come to a fork in the path, which now has you facing back towards Hout Bay. Take the level left-hand fork. To continue up would take you to the top of the rise and eventually (four hours later) to Constantia Nek. The level path will soon take you under an old fence, over piles of black manganese ore (looking for all the world like lumps of coal) and then to the gaping entrance of No. 7 shaft.

Of the eight shafts that make up Hout Bay's manganese mine, this has the most impressive entrance by far. It must be all of 15 m high and 3 m wide. However, don't judge a shaft by its entrance: somewhat disappointingly, it penetrates only 20 m into the mountain. You don't even need a torch.

To reach the deepest shaft you will need more time than the two hours allocated to this walk. If you have extra time to spare and curiosity is getting the better of you, scramble up on the Hout Bay side of No. 7. The No. 4 shaft you are looking for is about 100 m above and directly in line with No. 7. The entrance to No. 4 is large although partly hidden by undergrowth. In the entrance there are three holes, but two of these go straight down to No. 6 shaft below and should be avoided. The third hole is No. 4 shaft – at 84 m the longest of them all. You will need a torch to explore it. Even though at the time of writing there were no hidden holes to fall into in the dark, you do enter at your own risk. Also avoid winter when it could be wet and slippery.

Considering the primitive tools available in 1909, when the shaft was sunk, it is a quite remarkable feat of tunnelling.

To return, simply retrace your steps.

Points of Interest

❁ After numerous attempts, 1909 seems to be the first year in which manganese was successfully mined and shipped out of Hout Bay. As it was found rather high up on the mountainside, an economical means of transporting the ore down to a wait-ing ship had to be devised. Chapman's Peak Drive had not been built in 1909, so a jetty was built along with a chute to get the ore to the jetty. The remains of the chute are not so obvious, but the jetty is still there for all to see.

❁ The primitive and often rather ineffective chute was over 750 m in length and must have been quite impressive in full cry. However, all didn't go as the designers would have liked, because the steep gradient often caused the ore to go out of control.

❁ A popular Hout Bay urban legend has it that the first load of ore went careering down the chute and straight through the bottom of the waiting ship. Whilst this might be a colourful and amusing story, it is simply not true. An examination of the angle of the jetty to the shore and its construction, shows up the story for what it is – a local myth. Early photographs show that the ore was transported along the jetty in cocopans, quite apart from which there is a notable absence of a sunken ship to substantiate the tale.

❁ The manganese content of the ore varied greatly. In some cases the iron content (which occurs together with manganese) made a mockery of any reference to a manganese mine. One assay in the largest shaft revealed ore with 43 per cent iron and no manganese at all. A combination of transport problems and the decreasing grade of ore caused the mine to close down in 1911, after only two years of operation.

21. BLACKBURN RAVINE

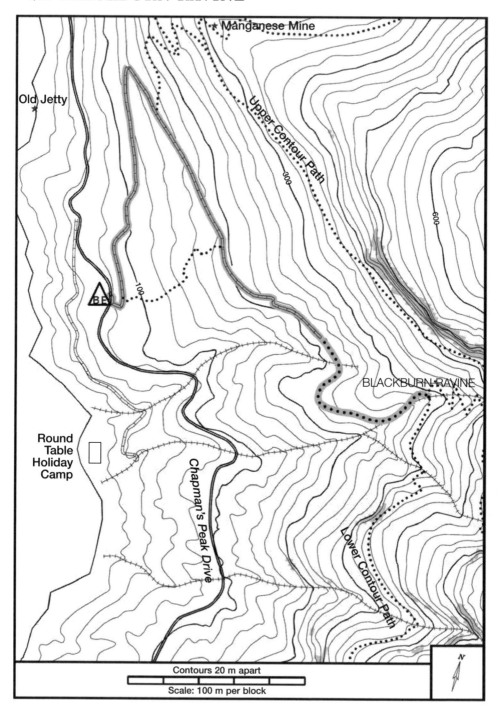

Manganese Mine

Old Jetty

Upper Contour Path

300

600

100

BF

BLACKBURN RAVINE

Round
Table
Holiday
Camp

Chapman's Peak Drive

Lower Contour Path

Contours 20 m apart

Scale: 100 m per block

N

Jan '05

Time: 1 hour 30 minutes

Distance: 4,6 km

Route: Return

Dogs allowed

Brief Description

A gentle walk mostly along a gravel forestry road without shade, to a delightful shady glen in an indigenous riverine forest. Have a refreshing drink of crystal-clear water from the weir, before returning via the same route.

Start

On Chapman's Peak Drive from the parking area 250 m beyond East Fort, where the gravel forestry road doubles back towards Hout Bay (1,5 km from the Chapman's Peak Hotel).

Directions

Walk up the gravel track in the direction of Hout Bay, before it doubles back on itself. Continue along the road for about half an hour from the start, until it narrows and degenerates into an overgrown path. Should you not be able to find the path, as it turns the last corner into Blackburn Ravine, scramble up the small clay embankment above you, and there you will find it. Stick with the path until it leads you into the densely wooded Blackburn Ravine and eventually to a small weir damming up the river to provide water for the old forester's cottage. You might have noticed this on the way up near East Fort, as well as the occasional exposed piping.

The huge 30-ton boulder in the river just below the weir came to rest here on 6 April 1985, after destroying all in its path on its way down from the cliffs above. Although fortunately no-one was there to witness it, that was the day the forester's cottage had its water supply suspended!

The elderly tree providing shade at the weir is one of many examples in this ravine of rooiels, otherwise commonly known as the red alder or butterspoon tree, so named from the "butterspoons" at the growing tip of each branch (*Cunonia capensis*). There are two paths which continue on from the weir. The path on the other side of the stream leads to Chapman's Nek and eventually Chapman's Peak. The path which climbs back and up the left bank (Hout Bay side) of the stream, crosses it higher up and eventually leads to the top of the mountain and the Silvermine Reservoir. However, both are a long distance away, and you should therefore retrace your steps to your car.

Points of Interest

❀ The so-called forestry road along which you have walked, doesn't appear to have a forest. However, it used to be a thriving pine plantation, established in 1906. It was eventually destroyed by fire in about 1960. Pines cause the soil to become acidic, which is much to the liking of fynbos, as evidenced by the profusion of pincushions, proteas, conebushes, ericas and many others which have re-established themselves in their rightful place.

CHAPMAN'S CONTOUR PATH

HOUT BAY

Time: 3 hours

Distance: 5,7 km

Route: One-way

Dogs allowed

Brief Description

The first half-hour is up a fairly steep ravine to reach the Contour Path high above Chapman's Peak Drive. Once at the higher level, it is an easy walk more or less on the level, dipping in and out of wooded ravines. The view of Hout Bay from on high is quite unforgettable. You will need to leave a car at each end, to avoid walking the 3,1 km back along Chapman's Peak Drive. An early-morning start will ensure maximum shade. The path is slightly exposed in places.

Start

Leave a car at the end of the walk, which is the parking area 250 m beyond East Fort on Chapman's Peak Drive (1,5 km from the Chapman's Peak Hotel, opposite Hout Bay beach). It is at the point where the gravel forestry road meets the tar. Then continue in a second car to the last picnic area before reaching the top of Chapman's Peak Drive. This is 3,1 km from the first car, on the left-hand side of the road, and on the last bend 750 m before the top.

Directions

Log steps lead from the left-hand side of the picnic area, and three minutes later cross a small stream. Once over the stream, go straight up the slope for 25 m before turning sharp left. You should now be on a well-worn old firebreak path, leading straight up the right-hand side of the ravine.

Twenty-five to thirty minutes after starting you will reach the top of the ravine and step onto a flat open area. A clear path branches off to the right. Ignore it and continue for a further 35 paces to come to a short wooden post and a meeting of four paths. To the right the path leads to Chapman's Peak, almost an hour away. Straight ahead the path leads to the top of the mountain and the Silvermine

22. CHAPMAN'S CONTOUR PATH

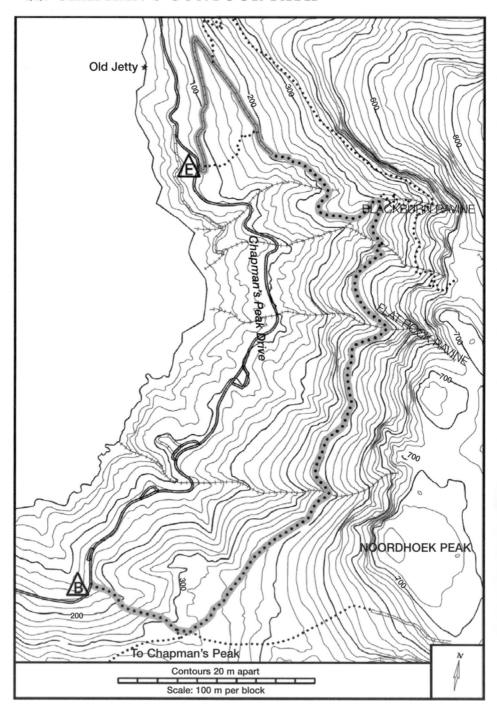

Old Jetty ⋆

E

BLACKBURN RAVINE

Chapman's Peak Drive

FLAT ROCK RAVINE

700

700

700

NOORDHOEK PEAK

700

B

200

300

To Chapman's Peak

N

Contours 20 m apart

Scale: 100 m per block

Nature Reserve. Your way is left. But first take a rest after your steep climb up, and be consoled by the fact that all the hard work is behind you.

The path to the left is not altogether obvious amongst the rocks of the crossroads. However, once you have walked a few metres over the rocks it becomes perfectly clear. About seven minutes along the contour, cross over a small stream where there usually seems to be water. Soon after, the full panorama of Hout Bay comes into view.

Thereafter the path dips into a couple of little ravines without losing height and then into a ravine, severely burnt by the January 2000 Great Fire.

I call this Flat Rock Ravine and it is a little over the halfway mark, so represents a good spot to stop for tea in the recovering indigenous forest. The next suitable spot (which is perhaps better because it has water) is Blackburn Ravine, but that is all of 25 minutes further on.

Once out of Flat Rock Ravine and around the corner, the path starts dropping and the path is very evident below you. From here you see Hout Bay at its best.

Blackburn Ravine was also densely wooded with indigenous trees before the fire, and it is encouraging to see them resprouting. You will know when you have got there by the little weir at the foot of a giant red alder (rooiels) tree. The pipe coming from it used to lead the old forester's cottage near East Fort, also destroyed in the 2000 fire. Be careful not to take a wrong turn here. Cross over the stream and immediately turn left down a steep section of path. To carry straight on once over the stream will eventually take you to the top of the mountain; not where you want to go.

Following the path down the right-hand bank of the ravine, follow the water pipe and avoid going back down to the river.

The path becomes broader and broader a while after leaving Blackburn Ravine, and eventually becomes a gravel road. This is probably the most uncomfortable part of the walk, as the gravel is composed of small loose rocks which are hard on the feet and ankles.

At the hairpin bend in the gravel forestry road, look down at the shoreline and notice the remains of the jetty which served to take away the ore from the Manganese Mine (see Chapter 20). Another ten minutes will get you back to your waiting car.

Points of Interest

❀ I have named this walk Chapman's Contour Path because it runs more or less parallel to Chapman's Peak Drive.

However, John Chapman had nothing to do with either of them, let alone Chapman's Peak itself.

❀ Chapman's Chaunce is the first known name of this beautiful bay. At 6.30 p.m. on 29 July 1607 the English ship *Consent* was becalmed at the entrance to the bay. Captain David Middleton decided to send a master's mate, one John Chapman, on a chancy mission ashore to see if a sheltered anchorage and fresh water could be found. As no charts existed it was, in the old English spelling, taking a "chaunce".

❀ Contrary to popular belief, Chapman's Peak Drive (originally known as the Hout Bay – Noorde Hoek Road) was not built by Italian prisoners-of-war. This would have been rather awkward, as Italy fought on the side of the Allies during World War I, the period during which it was built. The confusion probably arises from the use made of 5 000 Italian POWs to make a start with the construction of Du Toit's Kloof Pass between 1943 and 1945. But that was an entirely different World War.

❀ Chapman's Peak Drive was built with the help of convict labour. Construction started in 1915 from the Hout Bay end and more than a year later from the Noordhoek end. The two sections finally met in May 1922, when it was officially opened by the Governor-General, Prince Arthur of Connaught.

CONSTANTIA NEK TO KIRSTENBOSCH

23

Time: 1 hour 45 minutes

Distance: 6,1 km

Route: One-way

Dogs allowed on leash

Brief Description

A leisurely stroll through pine forest and fynbos which can be done at any time of the day or year, as it is mostly in shade and on the level. This is the first section of a contour path that continues all the way around the mountain to Kloof Nek. Have a car waiting for you at Kirstenbosch, and remember that the restaurant there serves an excellent breakfast or brunch.

Start

At Constantia Nek. A narrow tarred road leaves the Wynberg side of the picnic area and travels up for about 200 m before coming to a closed gate, with pedestrian access at the side.

Directions

Pass through the gate and walk along the gravel road for about four minutes, until you come to a fork. Take the left fork up. After a

further eight minutes or so, the road doubles back on itself opposite a steel road barrier. Don't double back, but rather carry on (to turn sharp left would take you to the dams and the Back Table along the so-called Bridle Path – actually a road). Carrying on along the straight you'll soon come out into the open, with splendid views of the Cape Flats and False Bay. A little koppie on the right offers a grandstand view. At this point the road does a sharp 90-degree left turn, and about 10 minutes later the black tiled roofs of the Cecilia Forest Officer's home come into view, as does a giant blue gum at a fork in the road. Take the more obvious right-hand fork and soon you'll come to a major intersection. At this intersection three roads and a set of log steps all come together. One road is behind you, one doubles back 180 degrees to the right to the foresters' cottages and one

91

23. CONSTANTIA NEK TO KIRSTENBOSCH

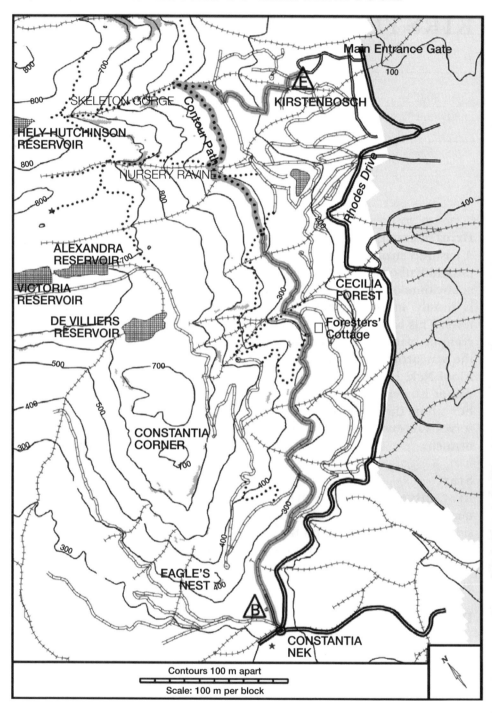

Main Entrance Gate

SKELETON GORGE

Contour Path

KIRSTENBOSCH

HELY-HUTCHINSON
RESERVOIR

NURSERY RAVINE

Rhodes Drive

ALEXANDRA
RESERVOIR

VICTORIA
RESERVOIR

CECILIA
FOREST

DE VILLIERS
RESERVOIR

Foresters'
Cottage

CONSTANTIA
CORNER

EAGLE'S
NEST

CONSTANTIA
NEK

Contours 100 m apart

Scale: 100 m per block

N

92

goes 90 degrees to the right. The steps on the left come down from Cecilia Waterfall. The way to go is the road going 90 degrees to the right.

Soon the road narrows to a path and shortly after it does a little U-bend around a small ravine, then climbing several log steps. Some fifteen paces on, turn sharp left up some more steep log steps. Do not continue on the level. At the top of the steps you will come to a notice at a fork in the path. Right and down will take you to the southern outskirts of Kirstenbosch Gardens. You need to keep left to continue on the Contour Path, but beware: having taken the left fork up, it almost immediately doubles back on itself. Do not double back, but rather carry on along the less obvious straight path.

Now you are out of the forest and into the fynbos. A few minutes further on you will meet a path coming up from Kirstenbosch. Ignore it and continue a few more metres to the bottom of Nursery Ravine (a sign set into the rock tells you that you have arrived there). Keep going along the Contour Path, now delightfully wrapped in indigenous forest. Ten minutes later you will reach the point where the Contour Path crosses Skeleton Gorge, and here another plaque announces "Smuts Track". At this point turn down the well-marked path which will lead you to the Kirstenbosch Restaurant some 15 minutes later.

Points of Interest

❀ Notice the pine trees are mostly of one particular type (*Pinus radiata*). They are commercially viable because all the knots appear at regular intervals where the branches radiate out from one point of the trunk. Also the main trunk is straight, as opposed to the pine commonly grown in gardens and particularly noticeable on Rondebosch Common (*Pinus pinaster*), which sends out large branches in any direction it pleases, making them commercially unattractive.

24. DE HEL

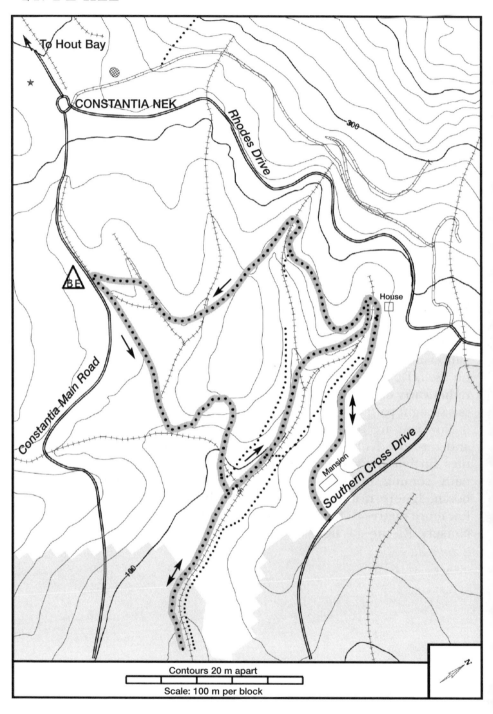

To Hout Bay

CONSTANTIA NEK

Rhodes Drive

300

BE

House

Constantia Main Road

Mansion

Southern Cross Drive

100

Contours 20 m apart

Scale: 100 m per block

N.

DE HEL

CONSTANTIA

Time: 1 hour

Distance: 4 km

Route: Return

Dogs allowed

Brief Description

A delightful walk through lush green forest in the heart of Constantia. Ideal as a light stroll in spring or summer when the trees are clothed in their finest green outfits. Mostly in shade and on fairly level ground.

Start

On the left-hand side, some 750 m down from Constantia Nek on the road to Constantia and Tokai.

Directions

Once through the gate at the start, turn right and follow the track downhill, running parallel to the main road. After a couple of minutes it swings sharply to the left and takes you down into the lush verdant valley. Near the bottom it narrows to a footpath and runs parallel to a stream. Shortly before it levels out, pass a wooden footbridge on the left, crossing over the stream. Ignore it and continue parallel to the stream, until you reach a second footbridge crossing the stream. Remember this point and continue along the level, past an open grassy area on the right. This is where the woodcutters, who worked this area in Van der Stel's time, had their basic accommodation. About 100 m further on, the path leads into a poplar forest where it eventually peters out. Negotiations continue with private landowners who have illegally extended their gardens onto public open space along the river bank. Sometime in the future, when the dispute has been sorted out, this path will continue to Gemini Way and Southern Cross Drive.

Retrace your steps from the poplar forest to the last footbridge. Cross over the stream here and begin a gentle climb up the left-hand side of a ravine. Shortly after the bridge, the path forks left or goes over another stream and up some steep steps to the right. Either path will bring you to the jeep track above, but the left-hand option is much gentler (see map), along a well-defined path through fairly dense forest.

Suddenly you are on a jeep track. Turn right and follow it, enjoying the interesting views down into the valley from which you have just climbed fairly effortlessly. It will be a surprise just how far above the valley floor you are.

Some 10-15 minutes after reaching the jeep track you will reach Southern Cross Drive and the signboard announcing the beginning/end of the trail, depending on which side you started from. At this point, turn around and retrace your steps as far as where you joined the jeep track. By continuing on it you will return to the start.

Points of Interest

❁ This was one of several *buiteposte* (outposts) established by the Dutch East India Company to supply timber for shipbuilding and repairs, as well as fuel. Continually burning fires were the order of the day for everyone from cooks to coopers. In those days they couldn't just turn a switch on or off, so the only answer was to burn loads of wood. This forest became one of the pillars on which the Cape's timber supply depended. Another *buitepost* was what is today known as Newlands Forest. But then it was called Paradijs. One line of thought goes that it was considered to be paradise by the woodcutters because it was close to the fleshpots of Wijnberg, not to mention the Tap House at Driekoppen (today a UCT residence is on the site). De Hel, on the other hand, was far from the basic pleasures of life, besides which it was right next to Simon van der Stel at Groote Constantia, allegedly the most cantankerous, ill-tempered so-and-so in the colony. So close to the devil incarnate had to be Hell. A far more likely, but less colourful theory on the origin of the name is the Dutch *De Hellen,* meaning The Slope.

❁ This verdant slope boasts about 250 species of plants of which unfortunately about one-third are aliens, including some horticultural escapees. The bird life is quite active for such a small area, with 66 species recorded.

SILLERY WALK

25

Jan '05

CONSTANTIA

Time: 10 minutes

Distance: 0,8 km

Route: One-way

Dogs allowed on leash

Brief Description

Take a stroll across a meadow and down an English country lane, with the pleasant and unmistakable smell of horses to complete the picture. And what more appropriate ending could there be to this shady stroll in the country, than a pub with an atmosphere that will make you stay longer than you should?

Start

On Constantia Main Road. From the Wynberg side, get to Christ Church, Constantia, where Ladies Mile Extension meets Constantia Main Road. 550 m further on from this intersection towards Constantia Nek is a broad green belt of open space on both sides of the road. On the right is a board marking the beginning of the Silverhurst Trail, and on the left a board which used to mark the beginning of the Sillery Walk until some mindless vandals broke it down. It is hoped it has since been replaced. If not, see the empty uprights as a damning indictment against that part of our human race which seeks only to destroy the constructive work of others. If you are approaching from the Constantia Nek side, the start is on the right, 450 m past the turn-off to Groot Constantia, just after crossing the Spaanschemat River.

Directions

From Constantia Main Road walk down the middle of the green belt which soon bends to the left. Just three minutes after starting you will reach the end of the meadow, and a wooden footbridge, sturdy enough to take a horse or two. Cross over the Spaanschemat River to a corner where two roads meet at right angles. Ignore the tarred road coming from the right and follow the gravelly lane to the left. This

97

25. SILLERY WALK

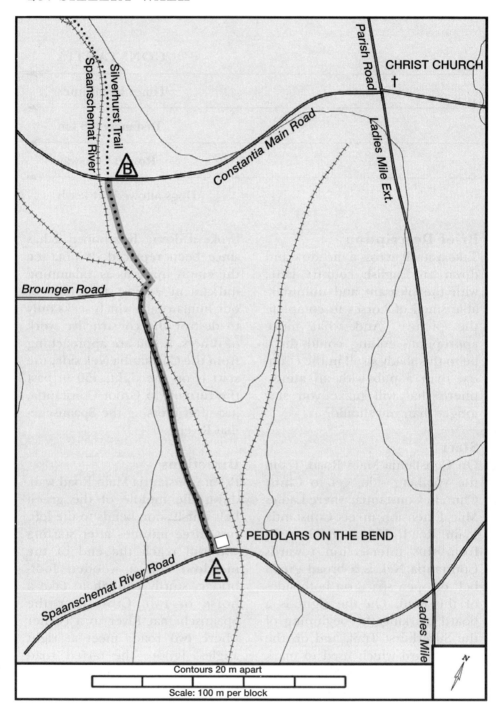

CHRIST CHURCH

Parish Road

Spaanschemat River

Silverhurst Trail

Constantia Main Road

Ladies Mile Ext.

B

Brounger Road

PEDDLARS ON THE BEND

E

Spaanschemat River Road

Ladies Mile

Contours 20 m apart

Scale: 100 m per block

N

will lead you under shade, past quaint cottages and later between a nursery on the left and stables on the right. Your destination looms. The Peddlars on the Bend tavern is a delightful finish to an easy hike – or should we not perhaps be honest and call the walk a means to an end!

Points of Interest

❀ Peddlars on the Bend occupies the site of what was originally the well-known Old Cape Farm Stall, and opened its doors in September 1993.

❀ Your dog's leash is not required for the walk, but for the drinks afterwards. Up until 2001 Peddlars on the Bend used to have a regular canine visitor called Boris. He belonged to the local vet and made the trip to the pub daily, unaccompanied. He had become quite a character, and the length of your stay was influenced by whether or not he liked your dog. But take your leash in case another canine character has taken Boris's place.

26. ALPHEN TRAIL

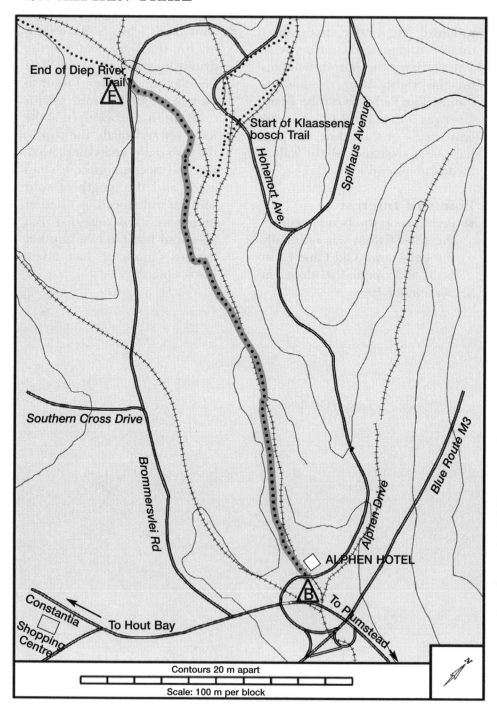

End of Diep River Trail

E

Start of Klaassens-bosch Trail

Hohenort Ave.

Spilhaus Avenue

Southern Cross Drive

Brommersvlei Rd

Blue Route M3

Alphen Drive

◇ ALPHEN HOTEL

B

To Plumstead

Constantia Shopping Centre

To Hout Bay

Contours 20 m apart

Scale: 100 m per block

ALPHEN TRAIL

Jan '05

Time: 35 minutes

Distance: 2 km

Route: One-way

Dogs allowed

Brief Description

This is one of a number of short trails laid out by the local council of Constantia Valley in 1994. It is difficult to imagine verdant hiking trails alongside river banks running smack through the middle of suburbia. But here they are. And you don't even realise you are in the middle of a built-up residential area.

Consider doing this trail in conjunction with the next three in order to make a not-too-strenuous and very varied three-hour circular walk, ending back where you started. By then, the sun will be over the yardarm and you could be excused for walking another 100 m to the Alphen Hotel. What finer setting in which to partake of the amber fluid, with the sun playing hide and seek through the oak leaves. A watering hole of unquestionable pedigree.

Start

On the main road from Plum-stead to Hout Bay, pass under the Blue Route freeway. Just beyond, take the turn to the right marked "Hohenort/Alphen". The start is indicated by a signboard just 100 m along this road. If you reach the Alphen Hotel, you have gone too far.

Directions

From the signboard the well-worn path takes you down this green belt running through the heart of an upmarket residential area. This is one of Constantia's green arteries. Near the start you cross over a small footbridge and, some 50 m further on, notice some trees alongside the path which have been painted grey. This is a poison which has been administered, not to discourage insects or fungus, but traditional medicine men who had been stripping the bark for muti. If this is done all around the trunk it has the short-term effect of killing the tree.

Somebody should tell them about the goose that lays the golden egg.

This walk in spring and summer is especially pleasing, with the trees clothed in many shades of lush green. There are numerous horticultural escapees to be seen along with many exotic trees, but they are mostly of the inoffensive kind. Fortunately Port Jackson and hakea have not found their way in here.

When you come to a notice describing the river restoration project, there is a long bridge crossing over the river to the right.

Here, the Alphen Trail forks into one of two options. Straight on will take you 10 minutes later to Brommersvlei Road and the start of the Diep River Trail.

If, however, you choose to cross over the bridge to the right, five minutes will bring you to an alternative end to the Alphen Trail, through a pine forest. Be sure to keep right at a couple of forks in the forest.

When you reach the Alphen Trail signboard, either turn around and retrace your steps, or if you wish to do the full four-trail circuit, continue 30 m further on to a tarred road (Hohenort Avenue). Turn right and walk 40 paces down the road to find another board marking the beginning of the Klaassensbosch Trail.

Points of Interest

✿ Should you take my advice and end the walk with some libation or other at the Alphen Hotel, you could well be drawn into the Boer and Brit to round off the walk. This delightful pub reflects in its name some of the history of the serene homestead and surroundings. The Boer War of 1899 tore the country asunder and, as in all civil wars, family loyalties were split. The Cloetes of Alphen were no exception. Henry Cloete, although of Dutch descent, acted as a British agent and entertained Lord Kitchener, amongst others, right here at Alphen. His beautiful wife, in true Victorian style, publicly supported him but privately had no intention of backing the British, and regularly passed on valuable information to the Boer forces. Messages were hidden in a hollow oak in the grounds for collection by Boer agents. So whilst quaffing an ale or two in the pub after your walk, realize that there's more to it than just a name.

KLAASSENSBOSCH TRAIL 27

CONSTANTIA

Time: 30 minutes

Distance: 1,7 km

Route: One-way

Dogs allowed

Brief Description
Entirely through forest which could be described as partly Afromontane and partly exotic. The trail starts off on the level and climbs ever so gently towards the end. The vegetation is superbly lush in spring and summer and you will snatch glimpses of some truly gracious homes through the leafy net.

Consider doing this in conjunction with the preceding and following two chapters, to make a three-hour circuit of it.

Start
Take the Plumstead/Constantia/Hout Bay turn-off from the Blue Route (M3). At the first traffic lights on the Hout Bay side of the freeway, follow the sign to Hohenort/Alphen. Drive past the entrance to the Alphen Hotel and along Alphen Drive for 1,5 km until it bears left into Spilhaus Avenue. Continue down what now becomes Hohenort Avenue for 0,5 km into a slight dip, where you will see the signboard announcing the Klaassensbosch Trail on the right.

Directions
Walk along the woodchip horse track to the right of the signboard and follow it for 100 m. Then bear left along a horse trail. After five minutes the path will take you straight over the embankment of a flood detention dam. There will be no water in it – unless of course there has been torrential rain. This is a safety measure to hold the flood waters back and prevent flooding further downstream in densely populated residential areas.

Go over the top and down into the empty bowl. The path will eventually lead you to the right-hand side of a magnificent property, between its green wire-mesh fence and a stream. Note the property's formal herb garden

27. KLAASSENSBOSCH TRAIL

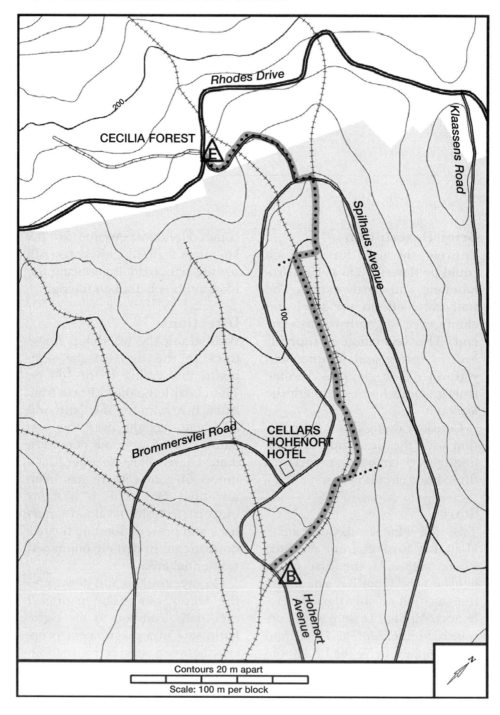

Contours 20 m apart

Scale: 100 m per block

next to the tennis court.

Follow the path until it comes to a T-junction at the garden gate of another lavish property. Should you need water, the owner has thoughtfully provided a push-button tap on the gatepost for the convenience of joggers and hikers. Turn right at this juncture. After crossing a couple of small footbridges the path spills out onto Spilhaus Avenue and the end of the trail.

For those wishing to continue on to the Cecilia Forest (see next chapter), walk 100 m down the road to the left then follow the sign saying "City/Rhodes Drive" up the hill for a further 400 m before coming to the parking area of Cecilia Forest Station.

Points of Interest

❧ The truly lush forest in spring and summer. The gardens and grounds of some of the finest homes in the Cape.

❧ *Klassenbosch, Klaasenbosch* and *Klaassensbosch* are but three spellings of this name found in the area. Historically the oldest spelling is *Klaassensbosch,* thereby giving it a respectability and correctness borne of age. The other spellings probably originated in a signwriters' workshop.

28. CECILIA FOREST

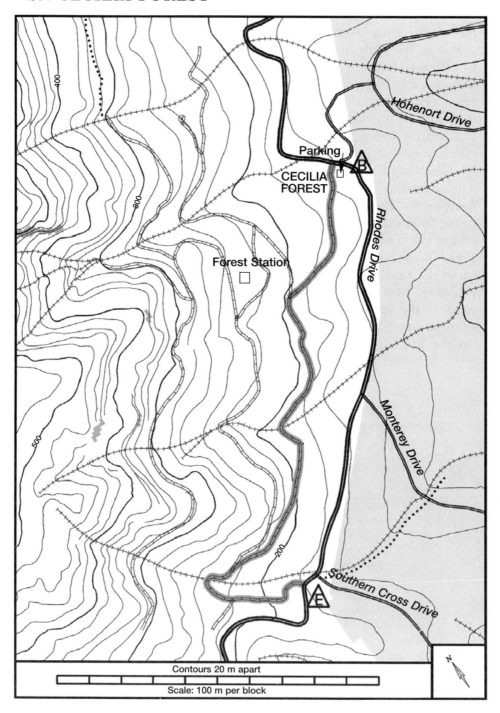

Contours 20 m apart

Scale: 100 m per block

CECILIA FOREST

CONSTANTIA

Time: 30 minutes

Distance: 1,9 km

Route: One-way

Dogs allowed

Brief Description

This was a fairly bland walk until an eighty-year-old pine forest was felled in 1997, revealing splendid views across the Cape Flats. It acts as a pleasant link between the Klaassensbosch and Diep River Trails for those wishing to do the three-hour/four-trail circuit starting from near the Alphen Hotel.

Start

At the parking area for Cecilia Forest on Rhodes Drive.

Directions

Follow the gravel road up for a few minutes until it does a sharp bend back on itself to the right. At this point, don't take the bend but carry straight on along a jeep track which runs more or less parallel to Rhodes Drive some way below.

After some ten to fifteen minutes another jeep track will join you from the right quarter. Remember it as a possible return route and continue your journey in the same direction past a pleasant stream 100 m on.

When you reach four abandoned buildings, take a left turn straight down the slope and head for the sound of the traffic on Rhodes Drive.

Return to the start by retracing your steps past the stream to the fork. Then along the upper jeep track via the Forest Station (see map).

If you wish to continue on the Diep River Trail, cross over Rhodes Drive and walk 100 m down Southern Cross Drive.

Points of Interest

✿ Cecilia Forest is not named after a Victorian maiden but after the man who owned it: Cecil John Rhodes.

✿ Rhodes Drive was not named in honour of the man, but quite simply belonged to him and ran through his vast estate.

29. DIEP RIVER TRAIL

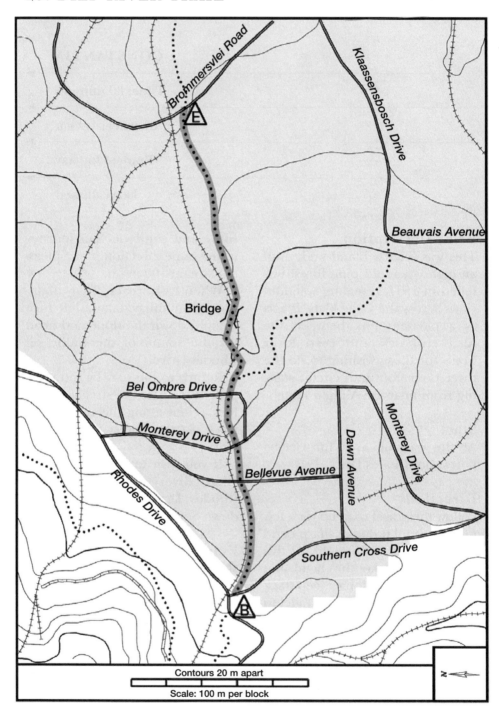

Contours 20 m apart

Scale: 100 m per block

108

DIEP RIVER TRAIL

CONSTANTIA

Time: 25 minutes

Distance: 1,5 km

Route: One-way

Dogs allowed

Brief Description

Another of Constantia's green arteries, this pleasant downhill trail, despite crossing over three tarred roads, still gives the impression of being out in the countryside. Think about combining this with the previous three chapters to do a three-hour/four-trail circular route starting and ending at the Alphen Hotel.

Start

100 m down Southern Cross Drive from Rhodes Drive. The signboard is on the left-hand side and just below the road.

Directions

Follow the clear path through pine forest before crossing over Bellevue Avenue. A couple of minutes later, cross over another road (Monterey Drive) where it meets the top of Bel Ombre Road. Five minutes on, cross a third road, which is the lower end of Bel Ombre Road.

At this point it is easy to go wrong, so take care. Having crossed over the third road, proceed 20 m into the bush, where you will come to a clear fork in the path. Take the narrower left fork. The more obvious, but wrong way, would be to carry straight on.

This narrower path will take you down to the river which it crosses on a short footbridge. A little further downstream you will recross the river on a 30 m long bridge through reeds and palmiet.

Another 10 minutes along a level grassy area beside the reeds will bring you to Brommersvlei Road and the end of this trail, marked by a signboard. Just over the road is the end of the Alphen Trail (one of two endings, as this latter trail is Y-shaped).

Points of Interest

✿ The authorities plan to create a bird sanctuary in the reeds surrounding the long wooden bridge.

30. TOKAI ARBORETUM

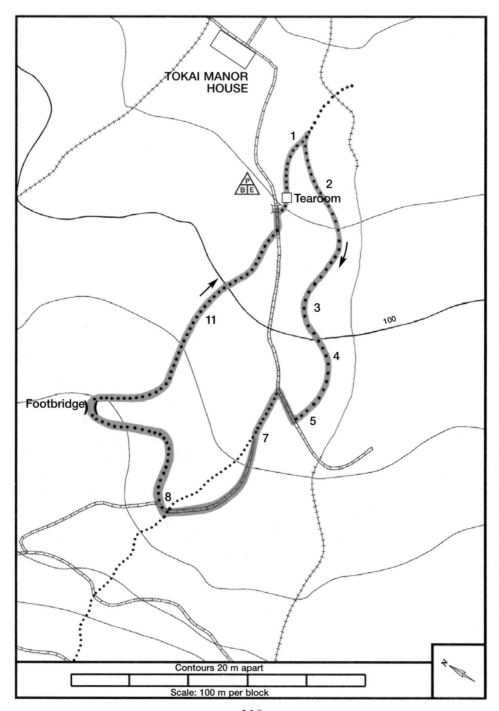

TOKAI MANOR HOUSE

Tearoom

Footbridge

1
2
3
4
5
7
8
11

100

Contours 20 m apart

Scale: 100 m per block

TOKAI ARBORETUM *Jan '05* 30

Time: 25 minutes

Distance: 1,6 km

Route: Circular

Dogs not allowed

Brief Description

If you think an oak is just an oak and a pine is just a pine – then think again. This arboreal United Nations is home to Turkey oaks, English oaks, Algerian oaks, Australian silky oaks, cork oaks and willow oaks. Not to mention Canary Island pines, Apache pines and a range of the more familiar ones. Then there's jarrah from Australia, giant redwoods from California, and different cypresses from Arizona, the Himalayas and Mexico. And much more.

The trees in this fascinating collection are each individually labelled, telling you from which corner of the globe they come. The circular route is along a clearly marked, well-defined path, without any great effort required. It's a walk in the park. A very different and diverse park.

Start

Leave the Blue Route (M3 motor-way) at the Retreat/Tokai turn-off. Then travel towards the mountain along Tokai Road for 1,5 km. Go 180 degrees around a traffic circle, continuing in the same general direction. The Steenberg Estate and golf course will be on your left. Keep straight on, ignoring Zwaanswyk Road going off to the left. A further 1,5 km from the circle (3 km from the Blue Route) will bring you to the gracious Tokai Manor House. Three hundred metres behind and to the left of the manor house is the Arboretum. At the entrance you will be required to make a modest donation towards the upkeep.

Directions

Before starting the walk, have a look at the Information display just inside the entrance. On the reverse side of it you will see an amazing map detailing the exact position of every tree in the forest, giving

111

each one its name. Pop into the nearby tearoom (Lister's Place) and for a modest fee pick up a tree guide and map.

The circular route (known as the Oak Leaf Path) begins in front of the tearoom. Follow the oak-leaf signs all the way (see map).

Walk to the left end of the tearoom and you will see a path leading off down the slope. Fifty metres on, it meets another path coming obliquely from the right. Take it to pass the back of the tearoom on your right. Just after reading oak-leaf sign no. 5, you will reach a broad track. Go down this to the right for 100 m, then turn up to the left (see map.) Soon after oak leaf no. 7 you will come to the junction of five paths. Oak leaf no. 8 shows the way. This will lead you to a little wooden footbridge, which you cross and now you are on the home stretch. Soon you will see the tearoom and be tempted by the smell of freshly baked scones and cream.

The Californian redwoods (*Sequia sempervirens*) planted in 1903 are a bit higher up than the circular walk will take you and if you wish to see them, this is a separate mission. Ask the gate attendant for details.

Points of Interest

❀ The Tokai Arboretum (tree garden) was established in 1885, meaning that many of the trees are well over 100 years old. It was started by Joseph Lister as a research project to establish which exotic trees could be commercially exploited in the Cape Colony. What we now have in forestry plantations throughout South Africa is a direct result of his research. Nursery Ravine above Kirstenbosch owes its name to him, for he established a similar arboretum at the top of the ravine, which became known as the Lister Nursery.

❀ Included in the 274 different types of trees to be found here, are an amazing variety of no fewer than 56 species of gums, 28 different pines and 21 oaks.

❀ There are plenty of indigenous trees also to be seen in the Tokai Arboretum, with yellowwoods (*Podocarpus* spp.) and wild peach (*Kiggelaria africana*) predominating.

❀ Although the original purpose of the Arboretum has been fulfilled, it has been decided to keep it going for its educational and historical value.

NOORDHOEK PEAK /Jan '05   **31**

SILVERMINE

Time: 3 hours

Distance: 6,4 km

Route: Circular

Dogs allowed

Brief Description

This walk is almost entirely along gravel roads, which makes it easy going. The view of Hout Bay from Noordhoek Peak is absolutely stunning and must rank as one of the most photogenic vistas in the country. If you plan to take photographs, get to the viewpoint in the morning, whilst the sun is still behind you. The view is well worth the effort. Take water and snacks.

Start

Drive to the top of Ou Kaapse Weg and from the direction of Cape Town, turn right into the north-western section of the Silvermine section of the TMNP. You'll be required to pay a modest fee at the gate, immediately beyond which you have a choice of taking a left turn or continuing straight ahead. Follow the tarred road straight ahead for 2,4 km until you reach a parking area just to the right of the Silvermine Reservoir wall.

Directions

From the parking area, take the gravel track which cuts across the valley below the reservoir wall. Once you have reached the end of the wall, bear left, following the gravel road on its gentle ascent. Keep to the main road and ignore the side roads to right and left. The road soon sweeps in a broad right-hand curve, climbing steadily. Within a few minutes you will come to a fork. The left fork is a dead end leading to a recently demolished lookout hut. However, the three-minute detour is worth it just for the view. You will be presented with a panorama of Simon's Town, Fish Hoek and Noordhoek.

From the fork, the road climbs steadily for some way before passing a dam on the right and then negotiating three sharp bends. Soon after the third bend you'll reach another fork, with a sandy track off to the left. This would take you down the mountain to

31. NOORDHOEK PEAK

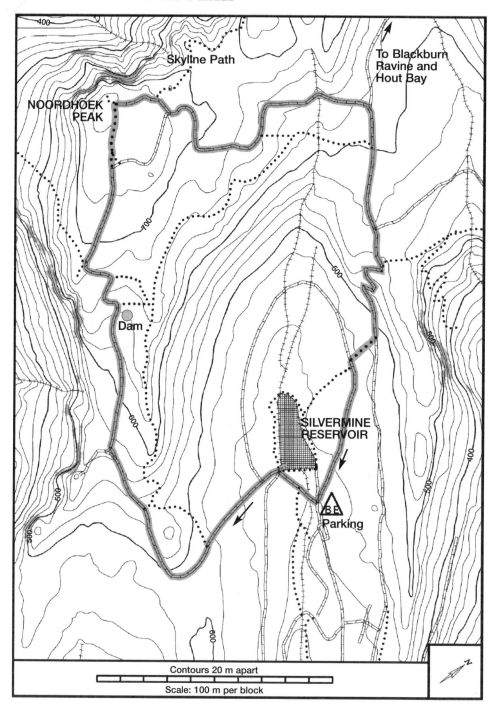

114

Chapman's Peak Drive, so ignore it and keep half right, along the gravel.

Approximately six to eight minutes further on you will come to a rocky cairn on the left-hand side of the road. Or if you miss it, a sandy jeep track 50 m further on, on the left. At either point leave the road and follow the footpath to a large stone pyramid, which can be seen a few hundred metres up ahead. The pyramid marks Noordhoek Peak. It will probably have taken you about one hour to reach the peak. Prepare yourself for a pleasant surprise as Hout Bay presents itself with an abruptness which is quite breathtaking.

On leaving Noordhoek Peak, don't retrace your steps but rather fork to the left, which will lead you back to the gravel road further down. The road now descends gently for about half an hour before sweeping to the right, into the home stretch. At this point

another road joins in from the left and behind, coming from the top of Blackburn Ravine above Hout Bay. Keep heading back towards the reservoir and soon you will come to a T-junction. Ignore the left turn and continue on straight where the road dips downhill and is reinforced with a double concrete strip. Soon it zigzags its way down the slope to the level of the reservoir. Don't be tempted to cut corners and add to the soil erosion problem.

You need to get to the darker of the two parallel roads (the one nearer the dam). It will lead you straight back to your car.

Points of Interest

✿ The name Silvermine is a complete misnomer. Although shafts were sunk in the area between 1675 and 1685 at the behest of the Here XVII, not one ounce of silver was ever found.

32. SILVERMINE RESERVOIR BOARDWALK

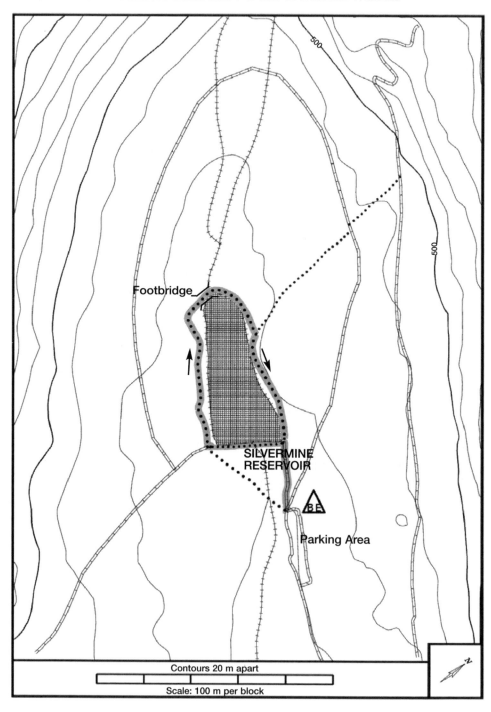

Footbridge

SILVERMINE
RESERVOIR

BE

Parking Area

500

500

Contours 20 m apart

Scale: 100 m per block

N

116

SILVERMINE RESERVOIR BOARDWALK 32

SILVERMINE

Time: 20 minutes

Distance: 1,1 km

Route: Circular

Dogs not allowed

Brief Description

A really easy stroll around the water's edge of the Silvermine Reservoir in a mountain setting. There are some ideal braai sites at the water's edge, in the most tranquil of surroundings. Swimming is permitted. Wheelchair friendly.

Start

Drive to the top of Ou Kaapse Weg and from the direction of Cape Town, turn right into the northwestern part of the Silvermine section of the TMNP. You'll be required to pay a modest fee at the gate, immediately beyond which you have a choice of taking a left turn or continuing straight ahead. Follow the tarred road straight ahead for 2,4 km until you reach a parking area just to the right of the Silvermine Reservoir wall.

Directions

From the far end of the parking area there are three routes: two gravel roads and a boardwalk between them. Take the boardwalk up to the top edge of the reservoir wall. You will be able to walk along the full length of the wall to the other side of the reservoir. It has railings and is perfectly safe, but if you don't fancy this, follow the road below the reservoir wall.

Either way, at the far end of the wall, turn right and walk along the boardwalk until you come to a footbridge crossing over the narrow far end of the reservoir.

Cross over the bridge and keep to the boardwalk on the return leg, passing through some excellent picnic and braai spots amongst the rocks.

Points of Interest

✿ The reservoir was built in 1898 by the old Kalk Bay Municipality to supply water for its residents, but is now used solely for the purpose of watering the Westlake golf course.

117

❀ The dark "Coca-Cola" appearance of the water is due to the presence of organic matter (mostly tannins). The colouring has been leached out from the roots and bark of vegetation growing in the water catchment area. It is perfectly harmless, but is removed from the water in the purification process, more for practical, industrial reasons than for anything to do with potability.

❀ Although the Great Fire of January 2000 did not affect the pine forest which surrounded the reservoir, the Table Mountain National Park took the opportunity of removing these aliens in the ensuing cleanup, to enable the fynbos to resume its rightful place in the Cape floral kingdom.

❀ The TMNP, together with volunteers, planted indigenous trees to the value of R50 000 around the reservoir after the pines were felled.

ELEPHANT'S EYE CAVE   33

Time: 2 hours 15 minutes

Distance: 4,8 km

Route: Return

Dogs allowed

Brief Description

This one requires a little more effort, but as half the walk is along gravel road, most of the upward climb is fairly gradual. The last 25 m before reaching the cave requires a little bit of rock scrambling, but it is no more difficult than climbing a short ladder. The view from inside the large cave is a picture, framed by the entrance.

Start

Drive to the top of Ou Kaapse Weg and from the direction of Cape Town, turn right into the northwestern section of the Silvermine section of the TMNP. You'll be required to pay a modest fee at the gate, immediately beyond which you have a choice of taking a left turn or continuing straight ahead. Follow the tarred road straight ahead for 2,4 km until you reach a parking area just to the right of the Silvermine Reservoir wall.

Directions

From the far end of the parking area there are three routes: two gravel roads and a boardwalk between them. Take the right-hand gravel road in the direction of the Constantiaberg mast. Three minutes later you should pass a stone building on your left (soon to be demolished). Another six minutes on will bring you to crossroads. A sandy track goes off to the left and 30 m on a road covered in short grass to the right. Take the grassy route to join up with a gravel road parallel to the first one. On reaching the T-junction where the grassy road meets the new gravel road, turn left.

This road will wind its way up the hill ahead for 10-15 minutes. At a point near the top you will come to a place where the road surface is reinforced with a double concrete strip. Leave the road here, along a path leading off to the right. This will take you to the

119

33. ELEPHANT'S EYE CAVE

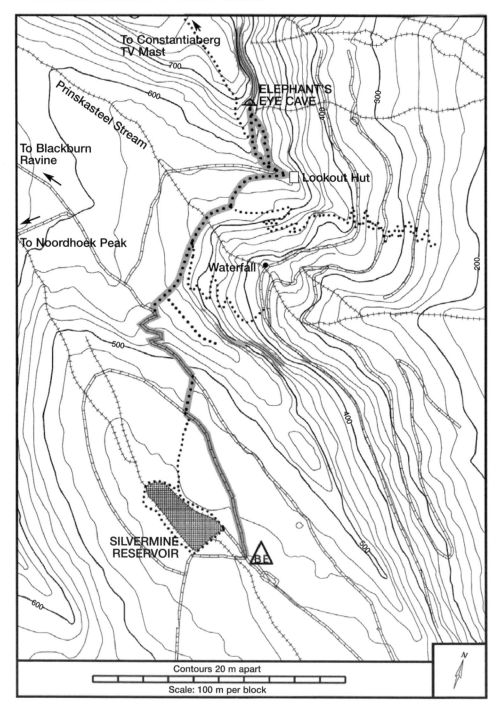

To Constantiaberg TV Mast

ELEPHANT'S EYE CAVE

Prinskasteel Stream

To Blackburn Ravine

To Noordhoek Peak

Lookout Hut

Waterfall

SILVERMINE RESERVOIR

Contours 20 m apart

Scale: 100 m per block

N

edge of a partly burnt-out pine forest, which it skirts to its far end, crossing over the headwaters of the Prinskasteel River. At some time in the future, this forest will be cut down to make way for fynbos.

Once over the stream, you will immediately see the Tokai Forest fire lookout hut on the skyline directly ahead. This is your next objective and will be reached in about 10 minutes. Once at the fire lookout hut, enjoy the superb sight on a summer's day of the rolling green vineyards of a verdant Constantia, laid out below you. Long may the developers keep their hands off them! Enjoy the majestic sweep of False Bay and in the other direction see if you can spot the upper cable station on Table Mountain, as seen from behind.

From here, Elephant's Eye Cave appears as a huge gaping black hole in the cliff face just above and to the right of you.

From the lookout hut, retrace your way down the log steps for 25 m, then turn right and follow the elephant signs to the cave.

Once in the cave, look out and see Princess Vlei on the left with Zeekoevlei in the centre, closely attached to Rondevlei and its wonderful bird sanctuary (the one with two small islands in the centre). The Strandfontein Sewage Works to the right is also a haven for birds of all shapes and sizes.

If on your return you don't fancy negotiating the little rock scramble just below the cave, it can be avoided by skirting around to the right and finding the path which leads down to the road without going back to the lookout hut. Get down to the stream and skirt the remains of the pine forest again, retracing your steps back to your car. Whilst skirting the forest, if you are tempted to pop down to see the Prinskasteel Waterfall, you will need to allow a further 15 minutes down and 20 to 25 minutes back up again. When returning to your car on the gravel road, avoid taking short cuts and thus adding to the already bad soil erosion.

Points of Interest

❀ From most parts of Tokai, this section of mountain takes on the shape of an elephant's head and trunk, with the cave in just the right position to be the eye.

34. SILVERMINE WATERFALL

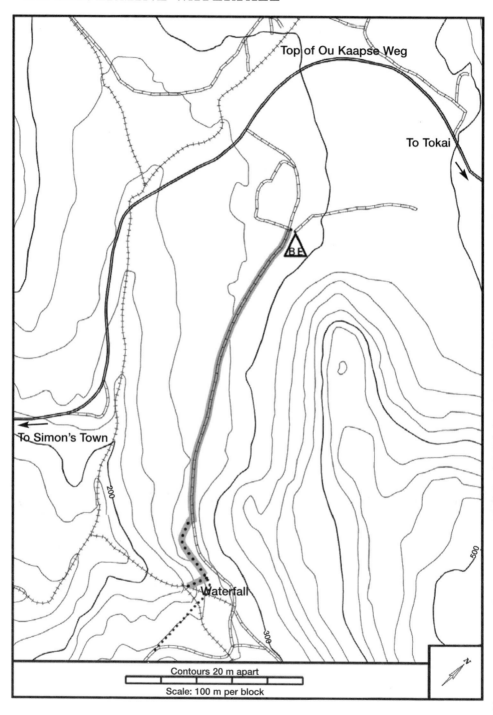

Top of Ou Kaapse Weg

To Tokai

BP

To Simon's Town

200

500

Waterfall

300

Contours 20 m apart

Scale: 100 m per block

SILVERMINE WATERFALL 34

Time: 45 minutes

Distance: 2,4 km

Route: Return

Dogs allowed

Brief Description

Mostly along gravel road to a most picturesque waterfall (especially in winter) set in an Afro-montane forest. It is a microcosm of South African indigenous trees – just a stone's throw away from what was alien pine forest, before the Great Fire of January 2000. Because of it's greater flammability and exposure, the pine forest (now the parking area) succumbed, and the indigenous forest survived.

Start

Drive to the top of Ou Kaapse Weg from the direction of Cape Town. On reaching the highest point, travel a further 500 m before turning left into the south-eastern section of Silvermine.

Look for the Table Mountain National Park signpost on the left and take the gravel road to the nearby parking area, where you will be required to pay a modest parking fee.

Directions

Walk around a boom at the far end of the parking area and ignore the gravel road coming in from the left. Keep to the track going half-right. This track descends ever so slightly for about 10 minutes before it begins to climb upwards for 200 meters. Just a few meters after reaching the top of the hill, look out for a marked path leaving the road on the right.

Take this path down with its steps made of logs and recycled plastic bars, but only as far as the long rock slab forming the top of the cliff face below. Don't be tempted to walk across the top of the cliff. Rather turn down, just before the rock slab. This will take you down steeply, with the help of a short ladder, to the bottom of the waterfall and into a magic grove of indigenous forest.

Return by the same route.

123

Points of Interest

✿ The dominant trees in this Afro-montane forest are rooi-els (*Cunonia capensis*) otherwise known in English as red alder or butterspoon tree. The latter name seems the most appropriate as the growing tips of each branch have an unopened double leaf closely resembling a butter spoon.

✿ Also common in this little waterfall forest are Cape beech, keurboom and yellowwood.

✿ Since the Great Fire of January 2000, plant species previously thought to have become extinct, have made a welcome reappearance in this area.

COASTAL WALK

Jan '05

35

MUIZENBERG

Time: 45 minutes

Distance: 3,4 km

Route: Return

Dogs not allowed

Brief Description

The Muizenberg – St James coastal walk is full of interesting local history, as well as rock pools and colourful bathing boxes. The leisurely stroll is entirely on the level on the concrete walkway along the water's edge. It starts at Muizenberg railway station and ends at St James station. You can return by the same route or along the main road to see some of the historic residences of the area. Or you could even catch the train back if the opportunity presents itself.

Start

Drive from Muizenberg Main Road to go under the railway line bridge. After passing under the railway line, take the second road to the right to get to the beachfront. Get onto the bricked parking area and drive as far as you can to get to the seaward side of Muizenberg railway station.

Directions

Starting opposite the station clock, pass under the archway announcing the Muizenberg – St James walk (the station building completed in 1913 is a national monument). Rough seas at high tide could result in a premature shower in places, so time your dash carefully! This is particularly so at the beginning of the walk in midwinter.

The path passes between the railway line and a thatched cottage right on the water's edge. This is Bailey's Cottage and was the seaside getaway of Sir Abe Bailey (1864 - 1940), a prominent politician, mining magnate and wealthy entrepreneur. It was built in 1909.

The route takes you between the beach huts that colourful postcards are made of. It continues for a short distance beyond St James station, before ending at a small beach. Now decide whether

125

35. COASTAL WALK

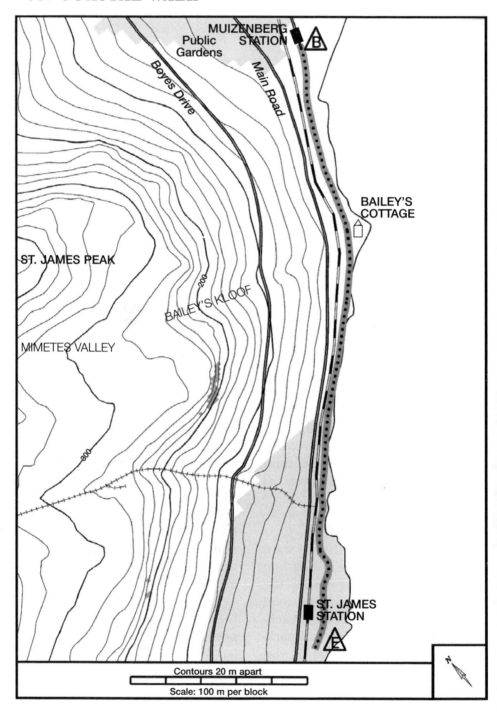

MUIZENBERG STATION

Public Gardens

Boyes Drive

Main Road

BAILEY'S COTTAGE

ST. JAMES PEAK

BAILEY'S KLOOF

-200-

MIMETES VALLEY

-800-

ST. JAMES STATION

N

Contours 20 m apart

Scale: 100 m per block

you want to return the same way, or along the main road to appreciate some of the historical buildings from close up.

Points of Interest

❁ The St James Hotel, opposite the station, was a very large house called "La Rivage" during the early 1900s.

❁ The largest mansion along the route, built in Spanish style with glazed green clay roof tiles, is the grand old "Graceland". It was built at the beginning of the First World War for the well-known Cape Town merchant, John Garlick.

❁ A little further towards Muizenberg is Rhodes Cottage. Empire builder Cecil John Rhodes died in the front bedroom in March 1902. He had bought it in 1898 after being besieged in Kimberley by the Boers. His health was failing (at the tender age then of 44) and he found the rooms at Groote Schuur were hot, stuffy and airless. He thought the "iodised salts" from the sea would benefit his health, so he spent most weekends here. It is a national monument and is now administered as a museum. Entrance is free.

❁ The Natale Labia Art Museum is a fine building in the Venetian style. It was erected in 1929/30 as the official residence for Italy's diplomatic representative to South Africa, Prince Natale Labia. It was donated to the state and opened as an art museum in 1988. As a satellite gallery of the South African National Gallery, it houses some fine works of art. There is a nominal entrance fee.

❁ Apart from Rhodes, Bailey and Prince Labia, other famous residents of the area were Sir Herbert Baker, architect; the Rev. Andrew Murray, pioneer of the Dutch Reformed Church and Robert Ardrey, American author.

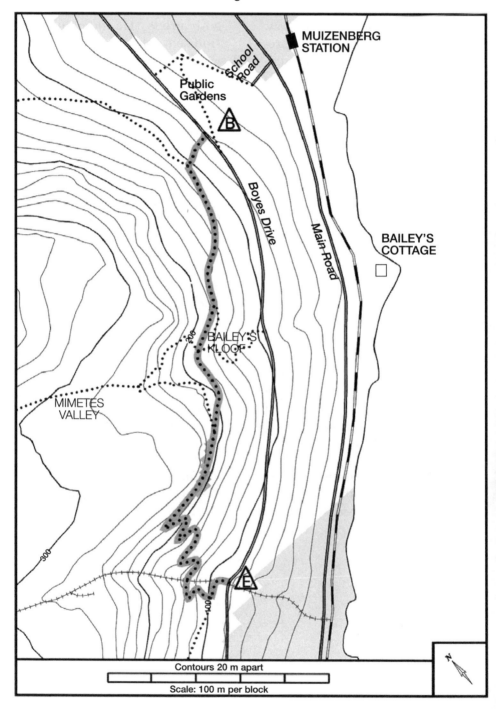

Contours 20 m apart

Scale: 100 m per block

MUIZENBERG – ST. JAMES HILLSIDE

MUIZENBERG

Time: 50 minutes

Distance: 1,5 km

Route: One-way

Dogs allowed

Brief Description

Some wonderful views of the longest beach in Cape Town. This walk requires a little bit of effort at the beginning and the going is somewhat rough underfoot, so wear the right shoes. The history and botany of the area is fascinating. Either stroll back along Boyes Drive (1,1 km) or have a car waiting at the end.

Start

On Boyes Drive, at a point directly opposite the clock tower on Muizenberg station. Some crude steps go straight up the mountain almost opposite a break in the fence, where a path comes up from the public gardens below.

If you leave another car at the end, it should be parked just beyond No. 110 Boyes Drive.

Directions

Climb up the steep slope from Boyes Drive for three or four min-

utes, before reaching a T-junction. Take a welcome rest and turn left towards Simon's Town. Another ten minutes of gentle uphill climbing will bring you to a fork in the path, at a flat rock slab. Keep right and slightly up, passing some steep steps on the right some three minutes further on.

You are now in Bailey's Kloof. Look down on Bailey's Cottage, a thatched-roof abode almost in the sea. It once belonged to Sir Abe Bailey (1864-1940), who featured prominently as a mining magnate and politician around the turn of the century. His grave, on a circular podium, can be seen about 50 m below Boyes Drive.

The path soon takes you to under a rock overhang, where Simon's Town suddenly comes into view. Five minutes on, the upward climb mercifully ends and the path starts a series of zigzags back down to the road. First two sharp zigzags, then a long straight level stretch, followed by four more zigzags to bring you just below a cliff face and overhang cave. Don't be tempted to cross the river at this point. Do yet another two zigzags before doing so. Spill back onto the road alongside the river.

Points of Interest

✿ You are looking down on the very spot where the Battle of Muizenberg took place two centuries ago. It's hard to imagine that this peaceful little corner of False Bay could have been the scene of such conflict. Picture eighteen English warships, with sails set like bulging chests, pounding the Dutch troops on the shore. The Dutch fell back and dug in at a place which consequently became known as Retreat. This battle was of immense significance in South African history, for it changed 150 years of Dutch occupation to 150 years of British domination.

✿ During early spring, on the downhill zigzag section of this walk, a flowering shrub called *Podalyria calyptrata* (ertjiebos) is in full flower and gives a spectacular display. It closely resembles a sweet pea in tree form.

ST. JAMES – KALK BAY HILLSIDE

MUIZENBERG

Time: 50 minutes

Distance: 2 km

Route: One-way

Dogs allowed

Brief Description

A gentle mountain climb with superb views of False Bay, including Simon's Town, Hangklip and Kalk Bay harbour nestling peacefully below. You will be surprised at the height to which you climb with very little effort. Highly recommended.

Start

On the bend just south of No. 110 Boyes Drive, almost opposite St James railway station. A TMNP signboard announces "Ou Kraal". Leave another car (or walk back) on Boyes Drive 1,5 km further south, at Ponder Road steps, opposite the Kalk Bay harbour entrance.

Directions

The broad path starts to the left of the river and climbs ever so gently in the direction of Simon's Town, whilst running parallel to Boyes Drive. You almost get the impression that Boyes Drive is dropping away below you, rather than you rising above it.

Listen for the clickety-clack of a passing train, and see the picturesque fishing harbour of Kalk Bay. Within half an hour you will suddenly spill out onto the end of a gravel track. There are some rather pleasant picnic spots in this rocky area known as Ou Kraal. Turn left at this T-junction and a few metres further on, take the fork downhill to a pleasant little watering hole called Weary Willy's under some indigenous trees and alongside a stream.

Cross over the stream and turn left to follow it on its gurgling way down the mountainside. About fifteen minutes down from Weary Willy's should see you back on Boyes Drive to your waiting car.

Points of Interest

✿ Flowering during spring from August to December is a pretty

131

37. ST. JAMES – KALK BAY HILLSIDE

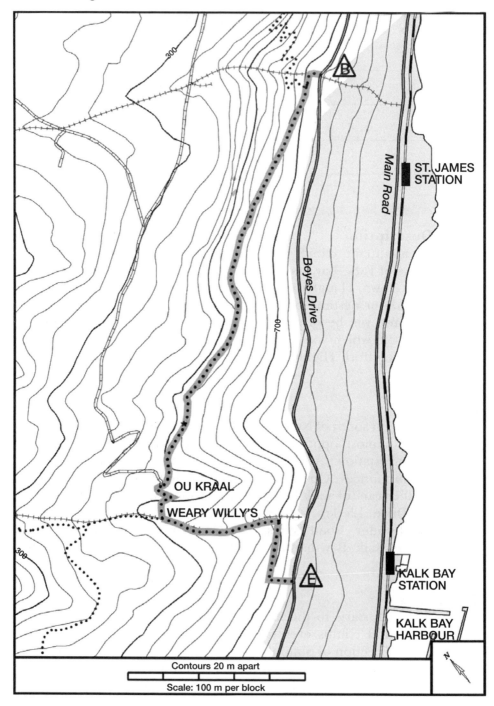

300

B

Main Road

ST. JAMES
STATION

Boyes Drive

700

OU KRAAL

WEARY WILLY'S

E

300

KALK BAY
STATION

KALK BAY
HARBOUR

Contours 20 m apart

Scale: 100 m per block

N

and very special little heath called *Erica urna-viridis.* (The Latin name means an erica resembling a green urn.) It is a delicate, almost white-greenish erica, sticky to the touch. What is so special about it, is that it occurs only on this mountain above Boyes Drive and nowhere else in the world.

✿ Kalk Bay got its name from the days of Simon van der Stel, when kilns were used to burn seashells to produce lime (Afr.: kalk) for mortar, to use in building throughout the Cape Peninsula. The limestone origins of the many caves in these mountains (67 in all) may have had some say in the matter.

38. LONG BEACH

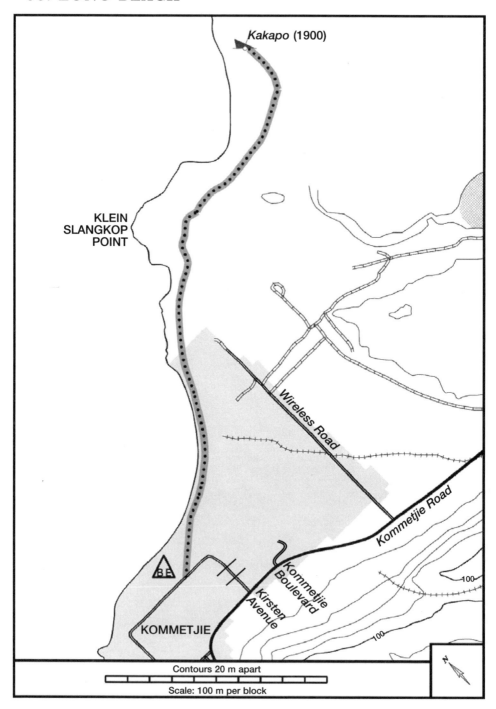

Kakapo (1900)

KLEIN SLANGKOP POINT

Wireless Road

Kommetjie Road

Kommetjie Boulevard

Kirsten Avenue

KOMMETJIE

100

100

Contours 20 m apart

Scale: 100 m per block

N

LONG BEACH

Jan '05

38

Time: 1 hour 45 minutes

Distance: 5,2 km

Route: Return

Dogs allowed

Brief Description

Along the beach between Kom-metjie and Noordhoek you'll be accompanied by the cry of gulls and the crash of the waves. The highlight of this walk is a fascinating shipwreck some way from the water's edge. Try to choose low tide for your walk, as the going is much easier on the firm sand of the intertidal zone.

Start

Once on the outskirts of Kom-metjie approaching from the Fish Hoek side, take the third turn to the right, into Kirsten Avenue, and follow the signs to Long Beach. There you will find a parking area adjacent to the beach.

Directions

Walk from the parking area to the water's edge. Soon after you start your walk in the direction of Hout Bay, you wouldn't be blamed for thinking you were at Arniston, with its quaint thatched and white-washed beach cottages. The architectural style is so "Cape Beach" that it almost begs to adorn a calendar. After about 25 minutes of walking along the beach you will get to a rock corner and your first glimpse of the wreck of the *Kakapo*, set back about 100 m above the high-water mark. It will first be seen as a black cylinder with a pole sticking up to the right. The cylinder is the ship's boiler and the pole is the rudderpost.

Forty-five minutes after starting you will reach the *Kakapo*. Notice how the rudder is still in the hard-a-port position, as a lasting reminder of the moment over a century ago when the captain desperately tried to correct his unfortunate error (see Points of Interest).

Points of Interest

✿ This steamship came ashore in circumstances that must have been most embarrassing to her master. The vessel was on its way from Table Bay to New Zealand one foul and stormy night in May 1900, whilst on her maiden voyage. As there was no Kommetjie Lighthouse in those days (first lit in 1919) the captain mistook Chapman's Peak for Cape Point and did a sharp left turn. With engines at full ahead and the assistance of a gale-force following wind and high spring tide, the ship was driven so high and dry onto the beach that the crew were able to walk off at low tide without getting their feet wet. Try explaining that to the shipowners and cargo under-writers back in London!

❀ The ribs of the *Kakapo* still stick defiantly out of the sand and give an indication of her size. Some of the plates forming the sides of the vessel were re-moved at one time and were used to prevent sand from blowing over the railway line at Fish Hoek.

❀ The boiler is quite fascinating. The three large holes at beach level are the furnaces into which the coal was shoveled. Two of them are still exposed enough to climb into. It was a fire tube boiler and the fire tubes, long since corroded away, connected the battery of holes you see.

❀ If you have ever wondered where a steamship at sea for a month or two got its fresh water from to feed its boilers, not to mention the crew, then look to the forward starboard (front right) side of the boiler. The upright cylindrical struc-ture is almost certainly the remains of the ship's evapora-tor. This was used to boil and distil sea water to produce fresh water.

COBRA CAMP

39

KOMMETJIE

Time: 2 hours

Distance: 5 km

Route: Return

Dogs allowed

Brief Description

An easy walk along a sandy jeep track to an abandoned World War II radar station. You will walk through some absolutely classic fynbos and be further rewarded with a stunning view which unexpectedly presents itself, looking down onto Kommetjie and the Slangkop Lighthouse. Return via the same route after exploring the three old blockhouses, each with a different vista. The place has an aura of both history and mystery about it.

Start

Travelling along Kommetjie Road between Sun Valley and Kommetjie, just after Ocean View township, there is a turn-off to the left marked "Cape Point/Scarborough". Take it and travel 2,0 km to the crest of the hill, where you will find a gate on either side of the road. The start of your walk is on the right-hand side at a notice board marked "Slangkop".

Directions

Take the sandy jeep track behind the gate. This area was heavily infested with a dense thicket of Port Jackson willow (*Acacia saligna*) until 1996, when it was cleared by the Kommetjie Environmental Action Group. It is most encouraging to see the return of the fynbos at the start of the walk. The now exposed graves on the left are those of the people who worked this ground when it used to be a farm.

The sandy jeep track climbs gently for about 20 minutes before reaching a high point where you are surrounded by classic fynbos. All three components are there – ericas, the reed-like restios and many members of the protea family. Spring is the best time to appreciate the area's 550 species of flowering plants. Bird-spotters are bound to see the fynbos specials – orange-breasted sunbird, greyback cisticola, rock martin, grassbird and others. Perhaps more com-

39. COBRA CAMP

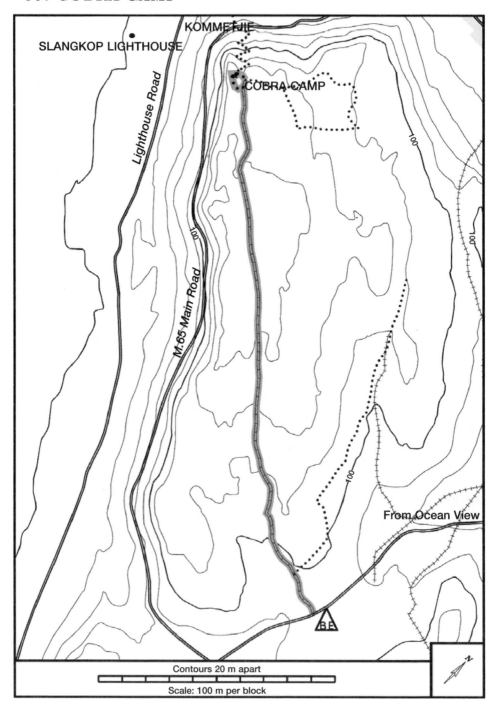

Contours 20 m apart

Scale: 100 m per block

mon here than most places is the ground woodpecker. Look out for him perching on a prominent rock.

Ten minutes after starting, you will pass an animal drinking trough and storage tank on the right. After about 45 minutes of following the jeep track, you will come to Cobra Camp. The derelict brick building in the foreground presumably provided accommodation for those manning the three concrete block-houses nearby. For the easiest path to the first blockhouse, go past the left of the building and keep to the same level, skirting around to the left. Suddenly you are presented with a wonderful view of Kommetjie village right below you. Also the Slangkop Lighthouse and an unusual aspect of Hout Bay present a pretty picture. I always enjoy views the most that come up on you all of a sudden. This is one of them.

A glance at the coastline gives away the origin of Kommetjie's name – the "little basin" which can clearly be seen. The rocky peninsula a few metres to the north of it is rather oddly called "The Island" and is a place where all our four species of marine cormorant are found. Also at different times of the year it is home to some really long-distance visitors – the arctic tern and the antarctic tern.

After exploring the cliff-hanging observation posts, return to your car via the same route.

Points of Interest

❀ Whoever heard of a lighthouse that doesn't light? Well, that's just what happened for nearly five years to the Slangkop Lighthouse (more commonly, but incorrectly known as the Kommetjie Lighthouse).

❀ After a series of shipwrecks in the area, including the *Maori* (see page 76) and the *Kakapo* (see page 135), it was decided to build a lighthouse right on the spot where the *Clan Munro* had met her end. It was completed in 1914, just days before the outbreak of "the war to end all wars".

This provided the authorities with a dilemma; for right next door was a military radio station, built in 1910. To light the light would have perfectly pinpointed a military target. So there stood this nonshining edifice, utterly useless. The lamp was finally lit in March 1919 after the ending of hostilities, and is still today the tallest lighthouse on the South African coast, as well as the fourth brightest (after Cape Point, Cape Agulhas and Cape Columbine).

❀ Passing ships, on entering a harbour, are required to pay "lighthouse dues" for the service they are provided with.

40. PEERS CAVE

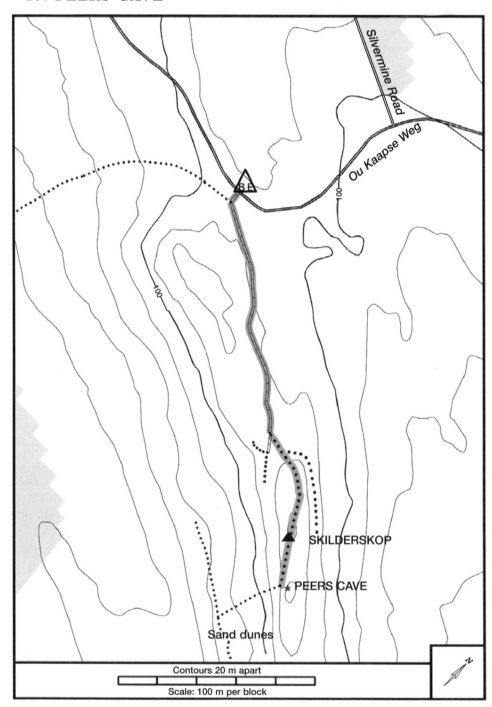

Silvermine Road

Ou Kaapse Weg

B.B

100

100

SKILDERSKOP

PEERS CAVE

Sand dunes

Contours 20 m apart

Scale: 100 m per block

N

PEERS CAVE

FISH HOEK

Time: 1 hour 20 minutes

Distance: 2,1 km

Route: Return

Dogs allowed

Brief Description

A walk mostly along the level, except for a short section of rock scrambling, to the home of the so-called Fish Hoek Man. He isn't exactly the new kid on the block, as he lived here as far back as 30 000 years ago. Allow about half an hour each way and 20 minutes in the cave, reflecting on what the neighbourhood looked like thousands of years back, when the sea filled this valley and the Southern Peninsula was an island. The shoreline was just below. You might even pick up a few seashells and reflect further on the food packaging used by the cave's previous occupants, while you eat your sandwiches and sip cool drink from their very different containers. Don't *you* leave them lying around as well! The cave is roughly 25 m wide at the mouth and 12 m deep. The ceiling averages six or seven metres above the uneven sandy floor.

Start

Drive down from the top of Ou Kaapse Weg in a southerly direction. After a little over 4 km the first turn-off to the right is Silvermine Road leading to Noordhoek. From this point, continue down Ou Kaapse Weg for a further 0,5 km. This will bring you to the crest of a hill, where the road bends to the right. On this bend there is a small parking area for about 10 cars. Park here.

Directions

At the left end of the parking area there is a sandy track to the left of a TMNP signboard. Follow this track and soon you will see the white trig beacon on top of Skilderskop directly ahead, telling you Peers Cave is below and beyond it.

Along this sandy track it is most encouraging to see the gradual return of indigenous vegetation, after the complete monopoly of Port Jackson willow (*Acacia saligna*) has been reversed by the introduction of the rust fungus (*Uromycladium* sp., see page 13).

After about ten minutes of walking along the sandy track it turns left and begins the gentle climb up Skilderskop.

About fifty metres up the slope, ignore a wood cutters path to the left (see map), and continue to the face of the rocks forming the koppie. Scramble up between and over rocks, to take you to the right-hand side of the peak and just below it. The secret here is to keep **close** to the rock face at all times. A deep cleft in the rock at one point might cause some doubt, as it appears to be a dead end. But turn right and go down ten meters at this point, before swinging left again and continuing to follow the rock face. Follow the most worn route over rocks and between trees, always staying on the Fish Hoek side and within a maximum of 10 meters of the rock face. You will come upon the cave suddenly, when you are level with a point about where Fish Hoek ends and Sun Valley starts, nearly opposite a large complex of playing fields.

At one stage a few years ago, this cave and valuable archaeological site was covered in mindless graffiti. It seems that its original Afrikaans name of Skildersgat (Painter's Cave) was taken literally. It was painstakingly cleaned up and restored to its natural condition in about 1994, unfortunately without the original Khoi paintings. It saddens me greatly to see that these sick people with their public toilet mentality are fouling the mountain again with their mere presence. Johan and Herman and Ibrahim (and Nevill, who doesn't seem capable of spelling his own name) – my message to you and all those like you, is go and seek help. You need it.

Retrace your steps to your car.

Points of Interest:

❀ Anthropologists from all over the world were all of a flutter in 1926 when Victor Peers and his son Bertie unearthed a skull in what was then called Skildersgat, a cave which now bears their name. The skull was identified by experts to be that of a 30-year-old male about 1,67 m tall. More importantly, he is estimated to have lived about 15 000 years ago, and was different in many respects from his modern descendants.

❀ A wealth of stone implements and other evidence of an earlier South Africa have since been unearthed.

❀ Prehistoric hearths composed of ashes left by ancient inhabitants have been carbon-dated to around 30 000 years old.

BRAKKLOOF RIDGE   41

Time: 2 hours 30 minutes

Distance: 5,8 km

Route: Return

Dogs allowed

Brief Description

A gentle climb up to the ridge above the end of Fish Hoek Main Road, through fynbos which has been regained from the onslaught of alien vegetation. Then through a burnt-out forest of what used to be a dense thicket of alien vegetation (mostly rooikrans and hakea). But don't be put off by the burnt-out forest – Mother Nature is rapidly replacing it with a wonderful display of colourful indigenous vegetation. The path goes along the ridge between Fish Hoek and Glencairn to a trig beacon marking the highest point on Brakkloof Ridge. Once at the beacon, return via the same route.

If you have two cars in the party, it is possible to shorten the walk to two hours by continuing down from the beacon in the general direction you have been travelling. This will eventually bring you to the end of Risi Road and your waiting vehicle.

Start

Make your way to the three-way traffic circle at the Simon's Town end of Fish Hoek Main Road. Assuming you are coming from the Cape Town end, turn right towards Kommetjie, and immediately on your left, just before a church, is a large off-road parking area. Leave your car here and go up some steps named Ravine Steps, leading off the far corner of the parking area.

If you plan to do the linear route you will need to leave a second car at the very end of Risi Road. Get there by driving from the church parking area at Ravine Steps for a distance of 1,5 km in the direction of Kommetjie, to a set of traffic lights. Then turn up Quarry Road, left into Carmichael and right into Risi.

Directions

Climb Ravine Steps to the top, crossing over two roads in the

143

41. BRAKKLOOF RIDGE

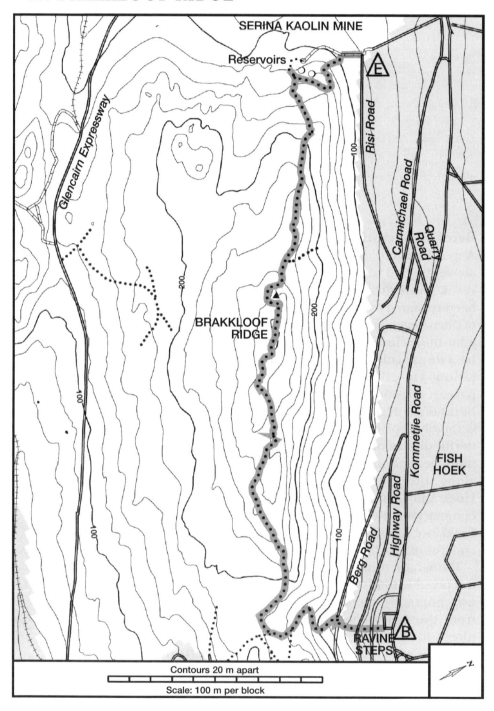

SERINA KAOLIN MINE

Reservoirs

E

Risi Road

Carmichael Road

Quarry Road

Glencairn Expressway

200

200

BRAKKLOOF RIDGE

100

100

Kommetjie Road

FISH HOEK

Highway Road

Berg Road

100

RAVINE STEPS

B

Contours 20 m apart

Scale: 100 m per block

N

process. At the third road the steps run out and a path continues the upward climb at a CPNP sign saying "Elsies Peak". Immediately after going between a rather incongruous collection of two oaks and a large palm tree, you will see a public drinking fountain directly ahead. After refreshing yourself, turn right and follow the obvious stony steps and gabions gently climbing the slope. Soon it doubles back on itself at a bench and continues the upward climb. Keep right and twenty to twenty-five minutes after starting, soon after the path becomes sandy, you will reach a fork in the path. A nameplate on the left says "Elsies Peak" and another on the right shows you the way to "Path via Ridge to Beacon". Continue the upward climb along the Ridge path and five minutes later you will come to another parting of the ways, suitably labelled. A right turn will continue the upward climb to the ridge. It is a delight to see the dramatic return of fynbos to this mountain after many years of being completely overrun by alien invaders (mostly rooikranz and hakea). Fires in 1999 and 2000, with follow-up work by government and private organisations, made all the difference.

A group calling themselves the Fish Hoek Alien Vegetation Control Group worked tirelessly to turn the tide of the alien plant invasion. They must have been delighted about the fires, but much work lies ahead for them, pulling out alien seedlings before they re-establish themselves.

About 45 minutes after passing the stone sign to the ridge beacon, you will eventually reach it. From here you can see all of Fish Hoek and right through to Noordhoek Beach. Fifty metres before the beacon there is a T-junction. At this point you need either to retrace your steps to the beginning or take the path at the T-junction down, first briefly in a southerly direction and then westerly again, to get to a second car near the border of Fish Hoek and Sun Valley at the Serina Kaolin Mine. From the beacon to the second car will take about 35 minutes. About seven minutes after leaving the beacon, you will come to a fork in the path. Go left here and follow the cairns as the path winds its way down the slope through a burnt (but alarmingly resprouting "spider gum" forest), past and above two reservoirs near the end, and finally onto a gravel road. Turn right when reaching the road and this will lead you to the end of Risi Road and your waiting second car. This last section of the walk has become seriously overgrown with various aliens including Port Jackson, myrtle, hakea and spider gum. It is in stark contrast with the beginning of the walk and needs serious attention.

Points of Interest

✿ The Fish Hoek Alien Vegetation Control Group are an organisation of mainly retired pensioners who voluntarily offer their services to hack out alien vegetation, in order for the natural fynbos to re-establish itself. They have had spectacular success with this small section of mountainside and deserve every encouragement. However, without wishing to sound ungrateful or even cynical towards their sterling efforts, my personal opinion is that hack groups work well on small areas like this, but in the overall picture they barely make a dent in the national problem. The scourge of these alien plants (mostly imported from Australia) is a very serious problem. They rob us of vast amounts of water which would otherwise fill our dams (fynbos doesn't use nearly as much). And they are taking over the richest botanical region in the world. When one considers that a very high percentage of medicines originate from plant sources, imagine the effects on the world at large if just a couple of dozen plant species took over from where there used to be 8 500 flowering plants, some holding the key to cures for everything from cancer to Aids. The only real solution is biological control. See "A Floral Paradise under Threat" on pages 12-14.

ELSIES PEAK

Jan '04

42

Time: 1 hour 20 minutes

Distance: 2,3 km

Route: Circular

Dogs allowed

Brief Description

An easy climb to a mountain top overlooking Fish Hoek and Glencairn, with a panoramic view over the whole of False Bay. During August, September and October you will possibly even see whales breaching (jumping almost clear of the water and crashing down on their sides). And the fynbos is quite special here, having been rescued by a voluntary conservation group from certain annihilation by alien plant invaders.

Start

Leave the Glencairn Main Road at the turn-off to Kommetjie (M6). After 200 m turn right into Birkenhead. Proceed up the hill and left into Clan Stewart Street. After some 800 m along Clan Stewart, turn right into Golconda and continue past side streets to the very top. At the highest point of Golconda a small tarred track with a chain across it starts off up the mountain.

Directions

The tarred track soon cuts back on itself and becomes gravel. At the corner you will notice some steps, which are your return route. Walk along the gravel road for about five minutes. At a point about 150 m before a concrete reservoir there are some log steps going up to the right. Take them to the nek above. Just after reaching the top of the hill, the path forks. Go right, and a few minutes later come to a T-junction on the floor of the valley. Turn right again and you will soon arrive at the back of a quarry with lots of loose scree, before the path swings to the right again. Soon after another fork presents itself. Once again take the right option. Twenty-five paces on, you have yet another choice between the direct route and the scenic route. The scenic route is far preferable. Either way, it eventually swings over from the Glencairn side to the Fish Hoek side and joins

42. ELSIES PEAK

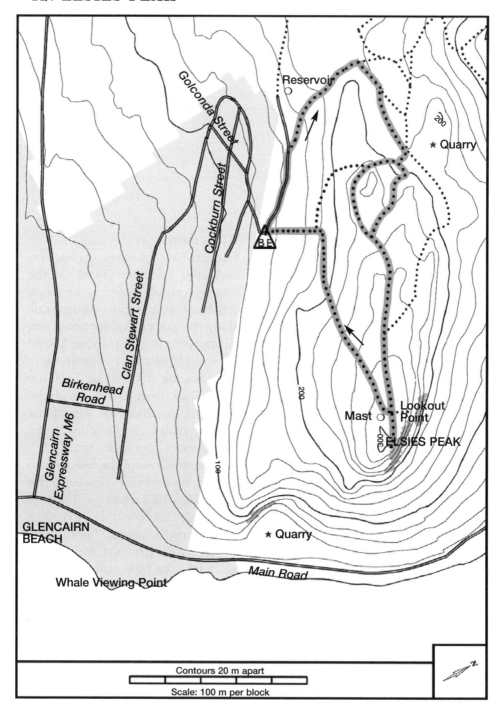

Contours 20 m apart

Scale: 100 m per block

another path coming up from the old quarry (see map). Keep heading upwards and soon you will see the Elsies Peak trig beacon and a 35 m high communications tower (used for cellphones, police security communications etc.).

Just before the mast, a side path goes off to the right (your return route) and five metres further on, another to the left, to a viewsite over Fish Hoek. The highest point and trig beacon is a few metres beyond the mast.

From here, enjoy the majestic sweep of coastline all the way around False Bay to Hangklip.

Retrace your steps from the beacon for about 100 m, then take the side path to the left. It soon begins descending the mountain in the direction of Glencairn, and within fifteen to twenty minutes will return you to your car.

Points of Interest

❀ A large whaling station was built at Kalk Bay in 1806, but was forced to close five years later because the whale population had declined so rapidly. Two centuries later, however, they keep returning each year in increasing numbers. The whales you will see between August and October are mostly southern right whales. Rather sadly, they are called "right whales" because they were the "right" whales to kill. They have a longer and more flexible baleen (food filter), which was once valuable to industry. Also, their carcasses floated and they were easier to tow and strip at sea.

❀ The immense size of these mammals has to be compared with more familiar animals to be really appreciated. Most of the southern right adults you will see, weigh the equivalent of 10 elephants. As large as that seems, however, it is nowhere near the size of the largest animal that has ever lived on this planet. The blue whale, which still occurs in certain parts of the globe, but not here, grows to over 30 m in length and weighs 140 tons – about the weight of 30 elephants.

❀ Southern right calves average 6,1 m in length at birth and weigh as much as five adult elephants. Whilst suckling they consume 600 litres of milk per day.

❀ Elsies Peak was not named after a lady, but a tree. It takes its name from the river which flows below it through the Glencairn Valley: the Elsies River. The river in turn took its name from the *else* or rooiels trees which used to line its banks. Not only was the name corrupted to *Elsie*, but the rooiels trees were displaced by alien plant invaders.

43. THE CATWALK

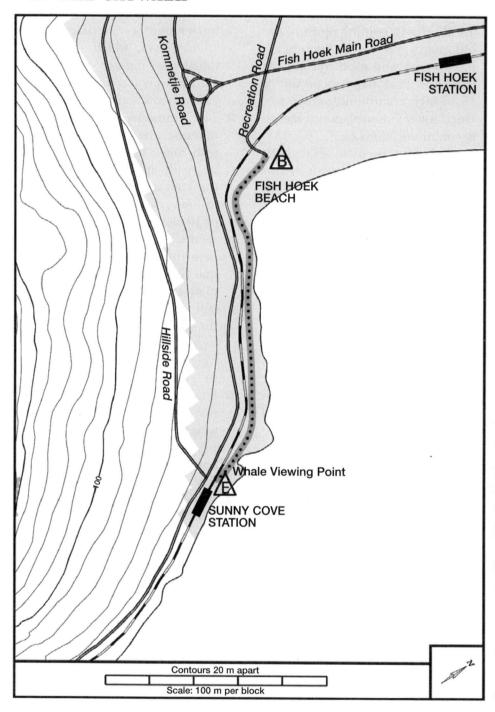

Kommetjie Road

Recreation Road

Fish Hoek Main Road

FISH HOEK
STATION

B

FISH HOEK
BEACH

Hillside Road

Whale Viewing Point

E

SUNNY COVE
STATION

100

Contours 20 m apart

Scale: 100 m per block

THE CATWALK

43

Time: 20 minutes

Distance: 1 km

Route: Return

Dogs not allowed

Brief Description

This leisurely stroll along the salty promenade between Fish Hoek beach and Sunny Cove station has benches strategically placed along the way to rest and enjoy the views. Gaze across False Bay to the Hottentots Holland mountains, stretching all the way to Cape Hangklip. It's even worth the odd swim here and there. Rock pools will provide fascination for young and old alike.

At the Sunny Cove end there's an excellent vantage point to view southern right whales, especially from August to October.

Start

At the extreme southern end of Fish Hoek beach.

Directions

Just keep strolling until you reach Sunny Cove station 500 m from Fish Hoek beach. Then turn around and return.

Points of Interest

✿ For many years one of Fish Hoek's main attractions has been its rocky coastline. After the railway line was built in 1890, the difficulty of negotiating the rough and tumbled boulders was overcome by using the railway line as a means of access. This was a fairly hazardous way of getting to your favourite fishing spot if you didn't have a timetable in your pocket, other than for the tides. So in 1931 the Village Management Board decided to build a cement path along the rocky coastline and completed it in 1933 at what was considered at the time to be an enormous cost of 715 pounds. It was named Jager Walk after a twelve-times mayor of the town, Herman Scott Jager. But it is far more often referred to as the Catwalk, which is defined as a narrow platform used in fashion shows. That figures!

151

44. KLEINPLAAS DAM

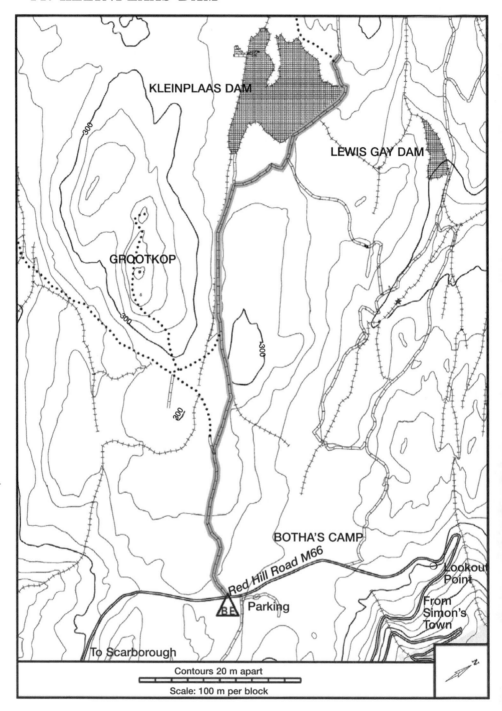

KLEINPLAAS DAM

LEWIS GAY DAM

GROOTKOP

BOTHA'S CAMP

Red Hill Road M66

Lookout Point

From Simon's Town

Parking

To Scarborough

Contours 20 m apart

Scale: 100 m per block

KLEINPLAAS DAM

44

Time: 2 hours 15 minutes

Distance: 7,8 km

Route: Return

Dogs allowed

Brief Description

This is a walk through one of the Cape Peninsula's fynbos hot spots. For anyone with a botanical bent this is a floral paradise, particularly in the springtime. Since the fires of 1994 and 2000 the veld has recovered well, and come back with a vengeance. There are numerous populations of rare plants, so the "no picking" rule applies even more especially here.

The route is along a fairly level jeep track the entire way to Simon's Town's water supply.

Start

On the main road between Glencairn and Simon's Town, 700 m before reaching Simon's Town railway station, turn right where the sign indicates the road (M66) to Scarborough via Red Hill. From this point measure 3,5 km to reach a large parking area on the left of Red Hill Road. This is a lookout spot well worth a stop to enjoy the spectacular view of Simon's Town and the naval dockyard. From the lookout spot, continue a further 1,3 km until you come to a sign on the left indicating the grave of Just Nuisance (see Points of Interest). Turn left here over a cattle-grid and immediately left again, to park your car.

Walk back to the road (M66) you have just turned off, and continue walking a further 100 paces up the road until you come to two large boulders placed at the beginning of a jeep track on the right. This marks the start.

Directions

Follow the jeep track through verdant fynbos for 15 to 20 minutes, after which time you will come to a fork. Take the right-hand option (see map). Soon the track begins to climb gently before dipping down into a valley, with Grootkop looming above you to the left. A single path joins the track

153

obliquely from the left. Continue along the narrow valley floor until you meet another fork, again taking the right option, over a slight hill. After a few hundred metres, turn left onto a gravel road leading a few metres further to the dam wall (see map).

At the time of writing, there was no route around the dam. I tried finding one (some survey maps show a myriad of paths that don't exist). In the process, I had an uncomfortably close encounter with a one-metre-long puff adder as thick as my forearm. Rather stick to the jeep track! Enjoy a drinks break on the shores of the dam and return along the same route.

Points of Interest

✿ Kleinplaas Dam was built in 1964 and the wall raised in 1970 to its present capacity of 1 300 Ml. It is built on the eastern portion of a farm that was known as Klein Plaats.

✿ Fish eagle occur at the dam, and the "call of Africa" can be clearly heard. The plaintive cry of the fish eagle never fails to leave me with gooseflesh.

✿ Just Nuisance has his grave a couple of kilometres from where you park your car. Just Nuisance, like Jock of the Bushveld, was immortalised in a book written about him. This Great Dane was more than just a dog. He was a Royal Navy mascot and did much to boost the morale of the sailors who came in contact with him. Born in 1937, he met his end in a car accident on his seventh birthday in 1944. But in his short seven years he became a legend, with stories still being told about him today. He was officially registered as an able-bodied seaman and posted to *HMS Afrikander*. His charge sheet showed numerous misdemeanours, including going AWOL whilst regularly taking the train ride to Cape Town. This was ostensibly to fetch drunken sailors back from the fleshpots of Cape Town, where he even had a bed at his disposal in the Union Jack Club. Like any good sailor, he regularly got into fights with mascots from visiting ships. He appeared in numerous publications including *Reader's Digest* and *Time* magazine.

GROOTKOP

45

Time: 2 hours

Distance: 5,4 km

Route: Return

Dogs allowed

Brief Description
A walk through the fynbos with a gentle climb at the end to the highest point in the area, with a panoramic view over the whole of the southern peninsula and False Bay. The second quarter of the walk is gently uphill, but well worth the effort, allowing you a bird's-eye view of the Kleinplaas Dam, Simon's Town's main water supply.

Start
On the main road between Glencairn and Simon's Town, 700 m before reaching Simon's Town railway station, turn right where the sign indicates the road (M66) to Scarborough via Red Hill. From this point measure 3,5 km to reach a large parking area on the left of Red Hill Road. This is a lookout spot, well worth a stop to enjoy the spectacular view of Simon's Town and the naval dockyard. From the lookout spot, continue a further 1,3 km until you come to a sign on the left indicating the grave of Just Nuisance (see previous page). Turn left here over a cattle-grid and immediately left again, to park your car.

Walk back to the road (M66) you have just turned off, and continue walking a further 100 paces up the road until you come to two large boulders indicating the start of the walk at the entrance to a jeep track on the right.

Directions
Some twelve to fifteen minutes along this jeep track you will see your destination creep into view: Grootkop, capped by a trig beacon. A couple of minutes later, look out for a fork. Take the option to the left (see map). Within a short while the sandy jeep track degenerates into a single path. After ten minutes along this path, all the time heading in the general direction of Grootkop, you

155

45. GROOTKOP

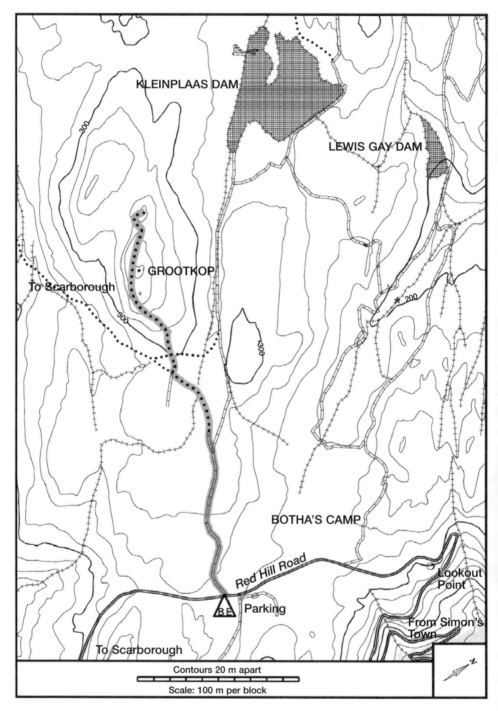

KLEINPLAAS DAM

LEWIS GAY DAM

To Scarborough

GROOTKOP

300

300

300

200

BOTHA'S CAMP

Red Hill Road

Lookout
Point

Parking

From Simon's
Town

To Scarborough

Contours 20 m apart

Scale: 100 m per block

N

156

will hit another jeep track at right angles. Turn right and just 50 m along cross over another path. Straight ahead is your way up Grootkop (see map).

Now begins a gentle climb for twenty to thirty minutes to reach the peak, along a path which winds in and out between rocks and crevices slightly to the left of a direct line. It is important constantly to keep an eye open for cairns, which show you the convoluted way up.

From the trig beacon at the top you can just see Seaforth peeping out, and to the left of that, amongst some trees, Botha's Camp (see Points of Interest). See also the large bowl above Simon's Town, which is Klawer Valley. This is naval property and closed to the public. On the right-hand side of the valley can be seen ammunition silos, on the left the signal school, and left middle a firing range – which will explain the alarming gunshots you might have been hearing. You might also have heard the dog school's noisy pupils. Kleinplaas Dam is right below you. On a clear day you will see Table Mountain, Constantiaberg and Chapman's Peak in the distance.

After taking in the view with tea, retrace your steps back to your car.

Points of Interest

✿ Botha's Camp – the South African Training Ship *General Botha* was moored in Simon's Bay from 1922 to 1942. She was there for the purpose of training young men for a career at sea as officers in the Merchant Navy. During World War II it was decided that she presented far too tempting a target for German U-boats, so the entire operation was moved ashore to Red Hill. In 1948 the college moved to Gordon's Bay and the site left behind became known as Botha's Camp. I had the honour and privilege of being a "Bothy Boy" during 1957 and 1958. Many a name amongst seafaring men were Bothy Boys, including war heroes "Sailor" Malan and J C Nettleton V.C. Alas, the college is no more, due to a lack of interest in a seagoing career among South African youngsters. It was certainly a way of seeing the world, as I had managed to visit 42 countries before I was out of my teens. Today, with modern air travel, that seems old hat. Or is this just an old-timer mumbling about the spirit of adventure missing in the youth of today?

46. ADMIRAL'S WATERFALL

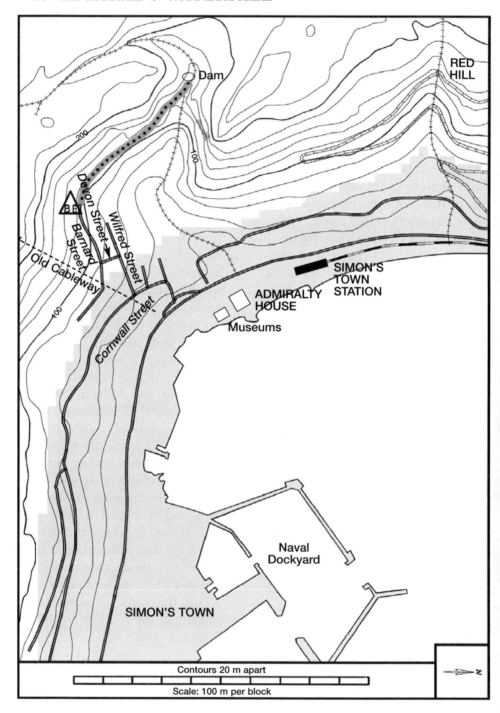

RED HILL

Dam

200

100

BB

Devon Street
Barnard Street
Wilfred Street
Old Cableway
100

Cornwall Street

SIMON'S TOWN STATION

ADMIRALTY HOUSE

Museums

Naval Dockyard

SIMON'S TOWN

Contours 20 m apart

Scale: 100 m per block

N

ADMIRAL'S WATERFALL   46

→

Time: 40 minutes

→

Distance: 1,1 km

→

Route: Return

→

Dogs allowed

Brief Description

A short easy walk to a rather small dam, but with stunning views along the way of Simon's Town and its naval dockyard from on high. A sprinkling of yachts moored in the bay, framed by mountains on either side, completes the picture. Best done after good rains on a sunny winter's day, to fully appreciate the waterfall below the dam.

Start

From the north, drive 500 m past Simon's Town railway station, and just beyond Admiralty House a road splinters off the main road to the half right and runs parallel to it, with large palm trees separating the upper and lower roads. Take this upper fork opposite a sign to the museums. After 100 m, at the crest of a hill, turn right to follow a sign saying "To Scenic Drive". Then up the hill and left into Cornwall Street as far

as the base of the cableway pylons. Then right into Wilfred Street, second left into Devon Street and finally right into Barnard Street. Continue climbing up Barnard Street for 250 m to the crest of the hill.

Directions

Park your car at the crest of the hill where it narrows considerably but remains tarred. Walk along this tarred section for two or three minutes after which it becomes a gravel path. Soon the path passes under a cliff face sporting Karoo-type vegetation, including wild rosemary (kapokbossie or *Eriocephalus africanus*). The seed heads of this very strong-smelling shrub are used by birds to line their nests, due to their soft cotton-ball texture.

The path climbs up fairly steeply for about 50 m, before levelling out again and bearing left into the

159

kloof to its small dam. There is a point where the path passes very close to the cliff face, presenting a long drop below. If you have a serious fear of heights, you will probably wish you had stayed at home. Have a tea stop at the silted-up dam, enjoy the magnificent view of the harbour and return via the same route.

Points of Interest

✿ The cableway seen on your drive to the start was used in the first part of the 20th century to ferry sick and injured sailors from the old Naval Hospital to a convalescent home on top of the hill.

✿ The Simon's Town Flora Conservation Group, under the dedicated guidance of Peter Salter, is doing its best to restore this area to its former glory.

Olea africana (wild olive) and *Olea capensis* (ironwood) previously filled this kloof. They can still be seen fighting their way bravely through the alien vegetation, composed mainly of ghost gums, Port Jackson willow and golden wattle.

✿ Looking down on the naval dockyard reminds me of the interesting origin of the expression "cold enough to freeze the balls of a brass monkey". In the old days of fighting ships, there was a brass triangle known as a monkey on the deck next to each gun. It was merely three strips of brass joined together, and its purpose was to contain the pyramid of cannon balls placed within it. In freezing conditions the brass contracted more than the iron, and the whole shooting match came tumbling down.

THE OLD MULE TRACK   47

Time: 2 hours 30 minutes

Distance: 5 km

Route: Return

Dogs allowed

Brief Description

This is probably one of the less easy walks in this book, only because it is uphill most of the way to the old Boer War blockhouses in the gap below Swartkop. But by the same token it is an easy walk down all the way back. The view of the False Bay coastline, the black-bearded proteas flowering in winter and the orange-breasted sunbirds make it all worthwhile. There is no water or shade, so keep this one for midyear, when the black-bearded proteas are at their best.

Start

Drive through Simon's Town, past Jubilee Square until you come to the police station at the other side of town. Then travel exactly one kilometre beyond the police station. This will bring you to the Simon's Town School. At the far end of the school ground, turn right up Harington Road for 200 m to the top. Then left into Jan Smuts Drive along which you drive for 300 m. Just after the rise of the hill, and before the road turns down towards the sea again (and becomes Churchill Avenue), there is a track going straight up the mountain. Leave your car at the bottom of the track, on Jan Smuts Drive.

Directions

Walk straight up the stone-asphalt track for 150 m until it forks, ignoring two tracks to the left. Take the right-hand fork onto gravel. A further 200 m along this eroded gravel track, it momentarily becomes tar and stone again, but only on the corner.

On this tarred corner, leave the track and follow the path which marks the upper level of an overgrown firebreak, towards Simon's Town. About five minutes along the firebreak path it seems to run out at a point opposite the middle of the school and above some ten-

47. THE OLD MULE TRACK

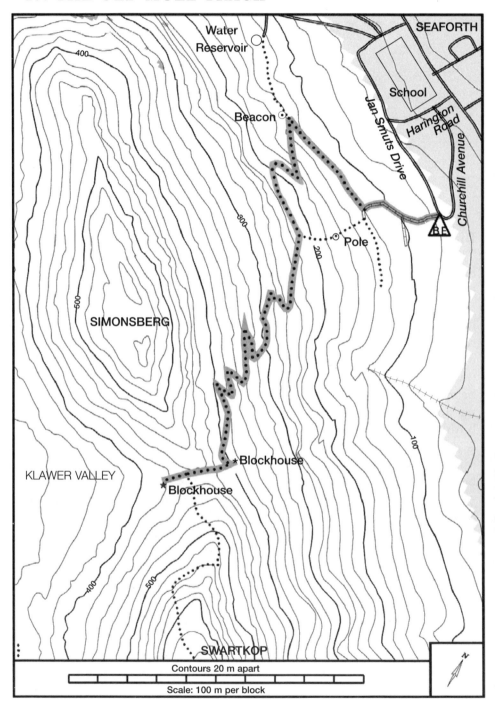

Contours 20 m apart

Scale: 100 m per block

162

nis courts. At this point, look for the remains of an old concrete trig beacon just above the path. Ten metres before this, the route leaves the contour path obliquely backwards and up. This marks the beginning of the old mule track.

Should you find yourself confronted by a concrete reservoir, you have overshot the mark by about 200m, and need to retrace your steps to look for the switchback. (See map).

The recent fires have taken their toll here. At the time of writing the fifth edition (winter 2003), the alien invader Port Jackson Willow (*Acacia saligna*) was coming back with a vengeance after it had been brought under control by the rust fungus (see page 13). Hopefully, with the help of biological control and follow-up, fynbos will win in the end.

As the path climbs, a view of the False Bay coastline begins to unfold. The magnificent dense carpet of proteas, pincushions, conebushes, erica's and restios that were wiped out by the fires are slowly but surely recovering. The path climbs relentlessly towards a blockhouse, just visible below a gully known as Blockhouse Gap.

On your way, look down on a large redbrick building block. This used to be the famous Rhodesia-by-the-Sea, frequented by Rhodesians on holiday in the 1950s and 1960s.

The path zigzags a few times to gain height near the end, and you should arrive at the blockhouse within an hour and a quarter of starting.

After resting and having tea at the first blockhouse, scramble up to the crest of the hill. In just three or four minutes you will come to the second blockhouse on the other side of the gap but, more interestingly, you will be presented with an unexpected view. You will be looking down on Klawer Valley, dotted with naval munitions stores, largely hidden from public view. Proceed no further than the second blockhouse, otherwise you will be trespassing on sensitive ground.

Between the two blockhouses a steep path leads up the mountain to the top of Swartkop. But that would turn a relatively easy walk into a strenuous one. So unless you are bursting with energy, retrace your steps to the beginning.

Points of Interest

❀ When Britannia ruled the waves, the dockyard below was nothing less than the Headquarters of the Royal Navy for the entire southern hemisphere.

❀ The Blockhouses have an air of mystery about them. They are thought to be relics of the Boer War, but no one seems to be quite sure, including the Simon's Town Museum.

✿ Roman Rock Lighthouse, seen straight out to sea beyond a large rock island known as Noah's Ark, was completed in 1867, after several years of thwarted attempts due to bad weather and only being able to build at low tide, when the rock was above the surface. It was electrified only as recently as 1992, when the SA Navy fitted underwater cable from the dockyard. Prior to that it was gas- and oil-fired.

✿ The nine-hole links golf course seen on the coast below is on the site of a prisoner-of-war camp used during the Boer War.

THE PENGUIN WALK 48

Time: 30 minutes

Distance: 1,7 km

Route: One-way

Dogs not allowed

Brief Description

A stroll along the coast from Seaforth, past The Boulders to Froggy Pond. The resident penguins at The Boulders are a delight. You will be required to pay a modest entrance fee to the area. Unless you wish to walk back, arrange for another car to be parked near Oatlands Holiday Village at Froggy Pond.

Start

Drive through Simon's Town, past Jubilee Square until you come to the police station at the other side of town. Then travel exactly one kilometre beyond the police station. This will bring you to the Simon's Town School, opposite which is the road down to Seaforth. Take this road down to a large parking area. Your start is from the bottom right-hand corner of the parking area.

Directions

Take the tarred road at the right-hand corner of the parking lot marked "Kleintuinweg" and walk along between the houses for about 200 m. This will bring you to the ticket office where you will need to purchase a ticket if you wish to go into the enclosed area to get a closer look at the penguins. The ticket office was converted from a South African Navy building which had an interesting function and was known as a Degaussing Centre. From it, leading into the water, were two heavy-gauge electric cables. These were connected to magnetometers under water, one placed in a north/south direction and the other facing east/west. When warships passed over them, sensors measured the magnetic signature of the vessel – which could well detonate a magnetic mine. The purpose of degaussing is to change the ship's magnetic signature to

48. THE PENGUIN WALK

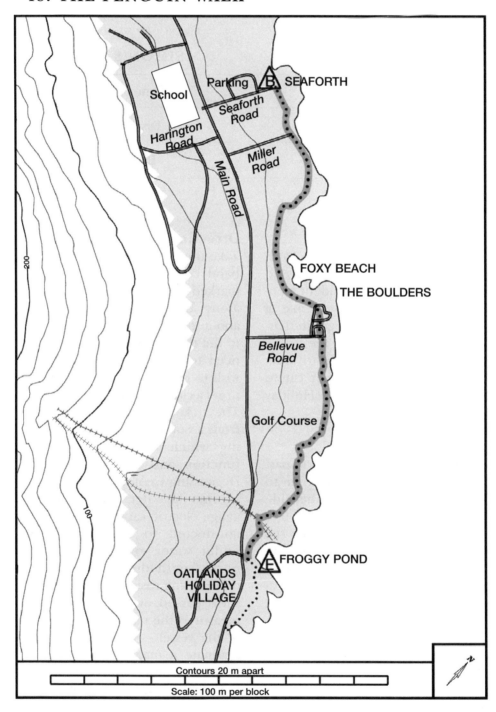

Contours 20 m apart

Scale: 100 m per block

the parameters required to avoid detonation of magnetic mines.

After passing (or visiting) the penguin enclosure and information centre, proceed along the tarred path and soon you will see jackass penguins anyway, nesting in the bushes just inside the fence. You could be forgiven if you thought there were a couple of donkeys hidden in the bush as well. The reason the penguins are called jackass penguins, however, is because their call sounds remarkably like the braying of a donkey. Ornithologists prefer to call them African penguins, as they are the only penguins that breed on the African continent (see Points of Interest).

The dense coastal bush alongside the path is interesting and particularly green at the end of winter, thanks to all the nitrogen from the guano. Among the plants are two species of wild olive, *Rhus* species, hotnotskersie, wild camphor and bastard saffron.

At about the halfway point of this walk you will pass another ticket office issuing tickets to people coming from the other direction.

After the second ticket office the path spills onto the parking area for The Boulders. Keep left and walk to the far end of the parking area, keeping close to the sea. Here the route goes over

lawn, along what is known as the "Burgher Wandelpad".

Aim for a large triangle on the rocks ahead. Your end point is just around the corner from there. After you have passed the last house, you will see a large wooden tripod almost opposite the triangle. The sandy path momentarily turns inland here, and suddenly you are rather rudely confronted by a public toilet. Turn left just before the toilet and back to the sea and a small beach. At the end of the beach, directly opposite the triangle, a steep short gravel path leads up to the edge of the golf course, and then down again. Do not stray onto the golf course, but skirt around the edge of it, finishing up on the main road opposite the Oatlands Holiday Village.

Points of Interest

❀ The African penguin population at Boulders Coastal Park has grown from one pair in 1985 to some 1 700 birds in 1996.

❀ They are present at the park throughout the year, with the highest numbers from February to April. The population is at its lowest from October to December.

❀ For a three-week period during the year they moult. This is to replace feathers which have been reduced in quality, due to continued exposure to sun and saltwater. As their feathers provide them with waterproofing, this means that for the three-week period they are unable to enter the water and therefore unable to gain access to food. To prepare for three weeks of starvation they engage in a feeding frenzy, resulting in the build-up of considerable fat reserves to carry them through the lean time. After moulting the birds are clean but thin, and need to feed for some weeks before they return to land.

❀ They tend to remain faithful to their mate and breeding place for life, which can be up to 25 years. The female lays a clutch of two eggs.

❀ The chicks are fed by the parents with a regurgitated fish porridge. At eleven to twelve weeks old they waddle off down to the sea and swim away without their parents. They are now alone and must support themselves, never having known what food looks like. Instinctively they have to recognize whole fish as food, and catch it. They are at sea for one year; but only if they learn to recognize the food they have never seen and without parents to teach them. Usually more than half die of starvation.

❀ This isn't their natural habitat. Normally they breed on the offshore rocky islands, which have built up layers of guano metres thick. They would burrow out a nesting place horizontally in the guano. This must make them one of the few creatures that build their homes in their own excrement! However, when bird droppings were elevated in status from the unmentionable to being a valuable fertilizer, they lost their homes. As we have destroyed their natural habitat, they are now burrowing into soil. What long-term effect the penguin droppings are going to have on the indigenous coastal vegetation, is debatable.

❀ Do not touch the penguins. You could be fined up to R3 000 for willfully disturbing them. If the authorities don't get you, the bird's powerful beak will.

THE SHIPWRECK TRAIL   **49**

Time: 2 hours

Distance: 5,8 km

Route: Circular

Dogs not allowed

Brief Description

A pleasant blend of beach and fynbos. The outward journey along the coastline takes you past two shipwrecks, then up a gentle hill and onto a fynbos-rich plateau overlooking the coastline for your return journey. Take water, sunglasses and a hat.

Start

Pay your entrance fee at the gates of the Cape of Good Hope section of the TMNP. From the entrance, drive 1,9 km to the first turn on the right, marked "Olifantsbos". Take the road to Olifantsbos, noting that the speed limit is 40 km/h. 10,6 km down this road will bring you to a parking area on the right, just before a boom across the road. This is Olifantsbos, and the beginning of two trails. Yours is clearly marked "Thomas T. Tucker Shipwreck Trail". The other one (Sirkelsvlei Trail) begins 150 m from the parking area, and is a long

lonely walk in the wilderness, to an interesting vlei which is kept topped up by an artesian well. If you feel like a long lonely walk in the wilderness you could combine the two trails, but you would need at least three hours. See directions further on if you wish to divert to Sirkelsvlei. For the Shipwreck Trail, start at the signboard.

Directions

Head south from the signboard and within 100 m the path forks. Take the left sandy fork rather than the stony right. Five minutes later the path forks again. This time take the stony right to get onto the shoreline. Now you will see a beach ahead which you need to cross. At the near corner of the beach is a house which used to be a farm-house, and is now known as Olifantsbos Cottage. It was converted by the authorities into an environmental awareness centre or "outdoor classroom" for study

169

49. SHIPWRECK TRAIL

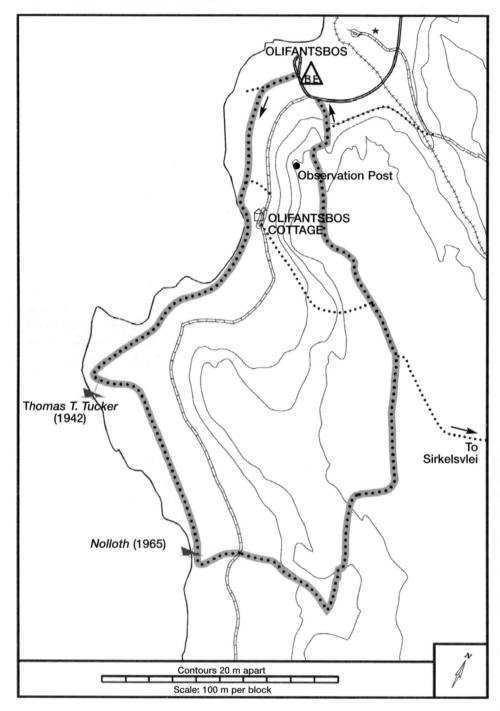

OLIFANTSBOS

Observation Post

OLIFANTSBOS COTTAGE

Thomas T. Tucker (1942)

Nolloth (1965)

To Sirkelsvlei

Contours 20 m apart

Scale: 100 m per block

groups, but is now used as over-night accomodation.

Cross the beach and then another small beach whilst, during the summer months, noisy black oystercatchers express their alarm at your presence (see Points of Interest).

You should reach the scattered remains of the *Thomas T. Tucker* about half an hour after starting out (see Points of Interest). Continue along the shoreline and just around the corner are two end rings of what was probably once the boiler of the *Thomas T. Tucker*.

Soon you will see another wreck a few hundred metres away. This is all that is left of the *Nolloth*, a Dutch-registered coaster wrecked in 1965. She was carrying a large cargo of liquor which attracted droves of people hopeful of picking up a little something on the beach. Alas, the Department of Customs and Excise had arrived first and set up camp. The ruddershaft and crankcasing are still clearly visible, indicating these are the remains of the stern section.

Leave the beach about 100 m beyond the *Nolloth*, where you will see a wooden pole where beach meets fynbos. Suddenly the terrain is entirely different. The path heading off inland starts behind the pole. The gentle climb to the plateau above swings first right and then left. At the top it heads

inland and some 20 minutes after leaving the beach, you will arrive at a signposted meeting of three paths. Take the left option marked "Car Park". If you really want a long lonely walk in the wilderness, you can take the path marked "Sirkelsvlei"; but allow an additional two hours to get back to your car. The "Car Park" route from here is only 25 minutes.

About three minutes along the "Car Park" path, avoid the left fork going downhill to the Olifantsbos Cottage. Look down and see the beaches you walked on earlier. Keep to the cliff edge and aim to the right of an old blockhouse and trig beacon on the horizon ahead. It is a clear path all the way past the block-house.

The blockhouse was built around 1940. This one was known as Bosch and was one of a number of observation posts providing coastal surveillance for the naval base at Simonstown. The Germans are unlikely to have tried to attack Simon's Town, with its impressive gun batteries, from the sea. The fear was that they might attempt a landing on the Atlantic coast of the southern peninsula and attack overland, from behind. Like its counterparts, the observation post was manned but not armed.

Five minutes after passing the blockhouse the path drops down a small ravine to the road and car park.

Points of Interest

✿ The *Thomas T. Tucker* hit the rocks in 1942. A glamorous version of her ignominious end was that she was attempting to avoid the unwelcome attentions of a U-boat. That fits, because she was carrying a cargo of tanks to aid the Allied effort in the war against the Third Reich. But Captain Bill Damerell, former Port Captain of Table Bay Harbour and maritime historian, thinks the wrecking was due to plain bad navigation.

✿ On your return route you might well see a herd of bontebok, which seem to be happiest around the parking area at Olifantsbos. The reason for their preference for this specific area is that it used to be a farm which, as a result of the farming activity, reverted to grassland. This is exactly what they want. As their natural habitat is Bredasdorp, where there is much more grass in the vegetation tapestry, this little spot seems like home from home.

✿ You are just as likely to see a troop of baboons in this area. **Under no circumstances should you feed them**, as you will almost certainly be signing their death warrant. Feed baboons and they will then come to expect it. Don't feed them and you could be attacked for not doing what they have come to expect. Attacks on humans not playing the game will follow your feeding them, as surely as the next step: a game ranger's bullet. Think about *that* the next time you want to feed a baboon.

✿ Just before the parking place at Olifantsbos is the largest stand of wild dagga (*Leonotis leonuris*) I have ever seen. Its bright orange flowers during the summer and autumn months cannot be missed. It is not narcotic and is no relation to dagga (*Cannabis*). It does however have a wide range of uses in medicine, with extracts curing everything from skin complaints to coughs.

✿ The African black oystercatchers that you would probably have seen on the coast are as interesting as they are rare. These distinctive birds have bright red legs, beak and eye rings, contrasting with black plumage. They are one of the world's rarest oystercatchers and have a world population of only about 5 000 individuals. Despite their rarity you are bound to see them here – usually in pairs. They pair for life and are quite long-lived

(30 to 40 years). During their breeding season (November to March) they are extremely vocal in defence of eggs or chicks and will not hesitate to tell you off, and attempt to lead you away from their off-spring. It is important that you comply, because for as long as they are trying to lure you away their eggs/chicks are exposed to the sun and predators. It's bad enough being rare – but exposed as well, is a bit too much!

50. HOEK VAN BOBBEJAAN

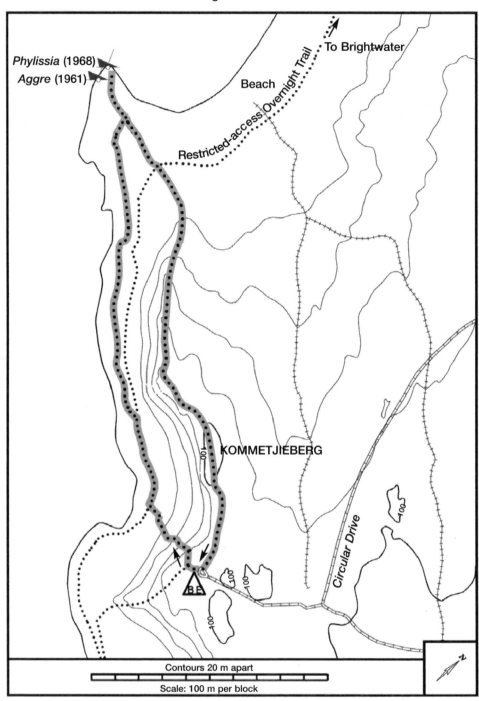

Phylissia (1968)

Aggre (1961)

To Brightwater

Beach

Restricted-access Overnight Trail

KOMMETJIEBERG

Circular Drive

B.F.

Contours 20 m apart

Scale: 100 m per block

HOEK VAN BOBBEJAAN

CAPE POINT

Time: 1 hour 45 minutes

Distance: 4,6 km

Route: Circular

Dogs not allowed

Brief Description

You will see an abundance of rock lizards and tortoises on this circular walk, and with the aid of binoculars, buck and sea birds as well. The outward journey hugging the coast takes you to a shipwreck, and the return journey along the top of a ridge offers an aerial view of the region, with buck visible on the open plains below. Wear lightweight boots or tackies, as the outward journey is mostly along soft sand. There is no water, so take some with you. Binoculars would be a bonus.

Start

Enter the Cape of Good Hope section of the TMNP after paying a modest fee at the gate. Drive some 4,4 km into the park before coming to a turn-off to the right marked "Circular Drive". Ignore this, and take the next turn-off to the right – also marked "Circular Drive". Follow the signs to Gifkommetjie.

Directions

At the Gifkommetjie parking area you will see a sign saying "Hoek van Bobbejaan three hour circular route". Don't be alarmed. The only way it could take three hours is on your hands and knees.

Take the path indicated on the left and within just a few metres it forks. Both forks lead down to the beach, but as your route is up the coast to the right, take the right-hand fork. A few metres on take another fork to the left. Don't go to the view site. That is your return route. Within ten minutes you will be at the water's edge. Follow the path parallel to the water's edge which in places is lost over smooth boulders. Within fifteen minutes you will come to a place where a rough sandy jeep track goes off to the left to continue following the coast, and the clear path carries straight on, following the line of cliffs on your right. Do not follow the path, but rather stick to the jeep track along the coast.

Eventually it will lead you to a rocky peninsula, the Hoek van Bobbejaan with its shipwreck. Do not proceed beyond the shipwreck, as you would be trespassing on a private beach.

Spend a few minutes contemplating the wreck whilst having a tea break on the rocks. Your way back is along the top of the ridge of Kommetjieberg, but getting up there is not nearly as strenuous as it might appear. With the wreck behind you, aim for a point on the skyline about 200 m to the left of the peak. It is mainly along a rough path, more or less heading in that direction. However, there are a number of such paths, so it would be confusing to try and be more specific. Just aim for that point on the skyline, and you'll pick it up soon enough. The route up to the peak is not well defined, but easy.

Once on top of the peak, look north, and you will be surprised to see Table Mountain. Kommetjie Lighthouse is also visible, and from on high you can look down on the plains below and probably pick out antelope. The wide open spaces with hardly a sign of civilization is remarkable when you consider how close this special place is to a major city. You are seeing what the strandlopers saw hundreds and thousands of years ago. From the top of the peak along a clear path on the ridge will take about 25 minutes back to your car.

Points of Interest

❀ The shipwreck is the remains of the I & J trawler *Phylissia*. The 450-tonner ran aground before midnight on 2 May 1968 and the crew were rescued by helicopter. The only beneficiaries of her 30-ton cargo of fish were the resident gulls and cormorants.

❀ The vast area of private land to the north of Hoek van Bobbejaan, including a long white beach and a scattering of buildings, used to be part of a much larger farm belonging to the Hare family. They tried to start their own private nature reserve, but their noble efforts were denied by poachers. As a result they presented the farm to the authorities as the nucleus of a wildlife reserve, on the condition that they could retain their seaside cottages at Brightwater. This fine gesture was one of the factors resulting in the formation of the Cape of Good Hope Nature Reserve in July 1939.

❀ Amongst the marine bird life of note along this section of coast are African black oystercatchers with their distinctive bright red legs, bill and eyes. Although endangered, they seem to be quite common here.

KANONKOP

51

CAPE POINT

Time: 2 hours

Distance: 4,2 km

Route: Circular

Dogs not allowed

Brief Description

Another leisurely and interesting walk in the Cape of Good Hope section of the TMNP, this one climbs gently through verdant fynbos to a hilltop on which is perched a cannon. The cannon will be reached in about 40 minutes. The route down is much steeper and more interesting, zigzagging its way through the remnants of an Afro-montane forest protected from the elements in a sheltered kloof. The descent will take another 40 minutes with a further 15 minutes along the tarred road, back to your car.

Start

Pay your entrance fee at the gate to the Cape of Good Hope section of the TMNP. The design of the entrance – for which the architect won an award – is highly controversial. Many people hate it, but others love it. Fortunately the entrance to the park is no reflection of what lies beyond.

6,5 km along the main road, after leaving the entrance gate behind, you will come to a sign pointing to the left indicating a turn-off to Bordjiesrif. Take this road for a further 1,2 km before coming to another sign to the left, this time indicating Black Rocks. Proceed up this road for 200 m to the top of the rise where you will find a small parking place on the right and the start of the trail clearly marked on the left.

Directions

Climb the log steps at the start and gently rise with the path, passing through some very vibrant-looking fynbos with restios, leucadendrons and proteas predominating. Look back on the tidal pool at Bordjiesrif and the two large crosses – replicas of those placed there by early Portuguese navigators.

In early summer the white everlastings (*Helichrysum vestitum*) are quite stunning and almost give the

51. KANONKOP

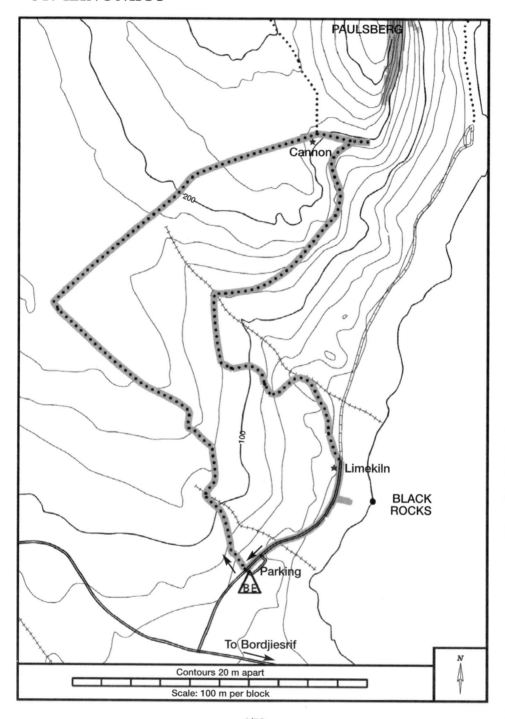

effect of the ground being covered in a thick layer of snow in places.

After about half an hour the path reaches a rocky ridge and swings around to the right. Soon the cannon will come into view, silhouetted against the horizon.

Rest at the cannon for a while and admire the all-round view. On a clear day you can even see Hermanus and Gansbaai, way beyond Hangklip on the other side of False Bay.

When leaving Kanonkop for the return descent, remember that the cannon points the way. Don't be tempted to take a more obvious path in the opposite direction, which would lead you back to the main gate past Paulsberg towering above you.

Five minutes after leaving the top there is a slight diversion from the main path to a splendid viewpoint. The route then winds its way down to the road which it joins at the site of an old limekiln, built around 1890. Follow the road in a southerly direction for 15 minutes whilst passing limestone cliffs, towering above some dense and healthy-looking milkwood trees. Your car is at the top of the rise.

Points of Interest

❀ The cannon is unlikely ever to have been fired in anger. From this spot it could only ever have been used as a signalling cannon to warn Simon's Town of the approach of hostile vessels. However, with the massive bulk of Paulsberg standing in the way, it is unlikely to have been heard in Simon's Town.

❀ Notice the considerable amount of white and orange lichen covering the rocks in the area of the cannon, looking for all the world like extravagant splashes of paint. These ancient and primitive organisms are in fact composed of two elements – an alga and a fungus living together for mutual benefit. This association is termed "obligatory mutualism", since it is thought that neither partner can live alone.

❀ Lichens are able to withstand severe drought, very high as well as subzero temperatures, and high-salinity conditions on the seashore. And yet they are extremely sensitive to air pollution. Often the presence or absence of these living organisms can be used as a measure of air pollution. They are very slow-growing, managing only about 1 mm per year. Some species are believed to live for up to 4 000 years.

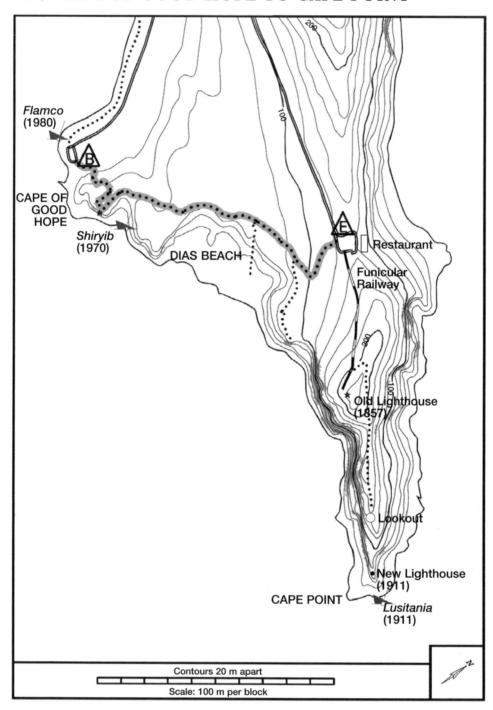

Flamco
(1980)

CAPE OF
GOOD
HOPE

Shiryib
(1970)

B

DIAS BEACH

E

Restaurant

Funicular
Railway

Old Lighthouse
(1857)

Lookout

New Lighthouse
(1911)

CAPE POINT

Lusitania
(1911)

Contours 20 m apart

Scale: 100 m per block

CAPE OF GOOD HOPE TO CAPE POINT

52

Time: 45 minutes

Distance: 1,6 km

Route: One-way

Dogs not allowed

Brief Description

A beautifully scenic walk with spectacular cliffs and a stunning beach looking as if it were the last unspoiled stretch of sand on earth. The first ten minutes of the walk will take your breath away, both literally and metaphorically. The steep log steps lead to a viewpoint which you will not forget easily. Once up the initial steep climb, the rest is a gentle gradient, with a lot of it being on boardwalks to protect the vegetation. You are almost bound to get very close to baboons, who don't seem to care less about your presence.

The parking area at Cape Point has a beautifully situated restaurant, where you could have a light meal after working up your appetite. If you haven't arranged to leave a car at the restaurant, the walk back is ten minutes less than it took you to come up.

Start

After entering the reserve at the main gate, drive 10 km down the main road towards Cape Point. Just after the 10 km mark, take a right turn marked "Cape of Good Hope". Most people seem to think the Cape of Good Hope and Cape Point are the same thing. Obviously, on this walk you will confirm this is not so.

The side road to Cape of Good Hope will take you 3,4 km to its end, and the beginning of the walk. A notice offers the profoundly useless information that you are now at the "south-western-most point of the African continent".

So what?

"Southern-most" or "western-most" I can understand might have some sort of significance, but this is rather like being half pregnant. I've even seen people standing proudly in front of the notice and having their photo-

181

graphs taken as if it were the very edge of the world. Avoid being seen too close to the notice.

Directions

The log steps at the start of the walk are steep (avoid sandy side paths), but only for about 10 minutes, when you will be presented with an incredible drop and a view of Cape Point normally seen by passing ships only. The boardwalk sections of the path can be seen from here, leading to the parking area and not the Cape Point Lighthouse.

So stop worrying about hard work from here on.

At about the halfway mark you pass way above the large and beautiful Dias Beach. Around this area there are usually baboons. I came across two on the path undergoing an intense grooming ritual, and had to walk around them as they seemed quite oblivious of my presence. The "nitpicker" had a look of intense concentration on its face and the "patient" wore an expression of total bliss, alarmingly human-like. **Do not feed the baboons under any circumstances**. You will be signing their death warrant. Baboons which have been fed by humans become aggressive and have to be shot. That seems dreadfully unfair; so just don't do it.

At the parking area there are shops, toilets and transport to the lighthouse.

Points of Interest

✿ Namibia has been called "the land God made in anger", but He must have been in a pretty grotty mood when He made Cape Point. According to the weathermen this is the most wind-exposed place on the entire African continent. The wind blows here at an average of 35 km/h for every hour over the entire year. That's windy. But so what? Do *not* avoid this place. You would be missing something very different.

✿ Cape Point has two lighthouses, but only the lower one is used. The old upper lighthouse was erected in 1857, but despite its height (211 metres) above sea level, was only visible in clear weather as it is often muffled by cloud. When the *Lusitania* was wrecked in foggy weather on the rocks below in 1911, it was decided to correct the mistake and build another lighthouse lower down. It is only 71 metres above sea level, but visible in most kinds of weather.

HIKING CLUBS

Absa Hiking Club
PO Box 1541
Somerset West 7129

Bellville Hiking Club,
PO Box 1089,
Oakdale 7534

Buite-Burger Club
PO Box 692
Cape Town 8000

Cape Province Mountain Club,
15 Stanhope Road,
Claremont 7700

Cumhike,
PO Box 12550
N1 City
7463

De Kuilen Hiking Club,
9 Mabille Road,
Kuils River 7580

Disabled Adventures,
15 Kingfisher Walk,
Pinelands 7405

Footloose Hiking Club
PO Box 4028
Cape Town 8000

Friends of Cape of Good Hope
PO Box 252
Simon's Town 7995

Friends of Hout Bay Museum,
4 Andrews Road,
Hout Bay 7806

Friends of the Liesbeek
PO Box 333
Rondebosch 7701

Friends of Lion's Head
PO Box 50335
Waterfront 8002

Friends of Silvermine
PO Box 283
Muizenberg 7950

Friends of Tokai Forest
PO Box 442
Bergvliet 7864

Happy Feet Hiking Club
PO Box 14661
Kenwyn 7780

Hotfoot Hobblers,
PO Box 6404,
Roggebaai 8012

Japtrappers,
PO Box 713,
Sanlamhof 7532

Meridian Hiking Club,
PO Box 50104,
Waterfront 8002

Mountain Club of South Africa,
97 Hatfield Street,
Cape Town 8001

Old Mutual Hiking Club,
PO Box 66,
Cape Town 8000

Peninsula Ramblers,
PO Box 982,
Cape Town 8000

Redwood Ramblers
19 Privateer Road,
Strandfontein 7785

Sanlam Hiking Club,
PO Box 1,
Sanlamhof 7532

Sapstap (SA Police Services),
32 15th Avenue,
Bellville 7530

SA Speleological Association,
PO Box 4812,
Cape Town 8000

Strollers Hiking Club,
43 Empire Road,
Ottery 7800

Thilo von Throta Stapgroep
PO Box 150
Gordons Bay 7150

Tirmanmak Hiking Club,
PO Box 825,
Parow 7500

Trails Club of South Africa,
PO Box 404,
Bergvliet 7864

Trotters Hiking Club,
PO Box 7329,
Roggebaai 8012

Tuff Trax Hiking Club,
PO Box 24511,
Lansdowne 7780

Viking Hiking Club,
PO Box 162,
Tafelsig,
Mitchells Plain 7785

INDEX

OTHER BOOKS BY MIKE LUNDY:

Twenty Walks around Hout Bay
    First Edition: 1985
    Second Edition: 1986
    Out of print: 1989

Best Walks in the Cape Peninsula
    First Edition: 1991
    First Edition, Second Impression: 1994
    Second Edition: 1995
    Second Edition, Second Impression: 1996
    Second Edition, Third Impression: 1997
    Third Edition: 1999
    Fourth Edition: 2002
    Fifth Edition: 2003
    Sixth Edition: 2005

Weekend Trails in the Western Cape
    First Edition: 1992
    Second Edition: 1993
    Third Edition: 1996
    Fourth Edition: 1999
    Fifth Edition: 2000
    Sixth Edition: 2003
    Sixth Edition, Second Impression: 2004

Armchair Hiking in the Western Cape
    First Edition: 1999

Co-Author of
Top Treks of the World
    First Edition: 2001

Adventure Gear to Climb Mountains for.

· SINCE 1933 ·

CAPE UNION MART

The Adventure Starts Here.

Call 08000-34000 or visit www.capeunionmart.co.za